PROFESSIONAL INVESTIGATION

E. ANIM-DANQUAH

authorHOUSE®

AuthorHouse™
1663 Liberty Drive
Bloomington, IN 47403
www.authorhouse.com
Phone: 1 (800) 839-8640

Published by AuthorHouse 10/25/2018

ISBN: 978-1-5462-6516-0 (sc)
ISBN: 978-1-5462-6515-3 (hc)
ISBN: 978-1-5462-6514-6 (e)

Library of Congress Control Number: 2018912613

Print information available on the last page.

DEDICATION

THIS BOOK IS SPECIALLY DEDICATED TO THE MEMORIES OF MY BIOLOGICAL FATHER, THE LATE SAMUEL KOFI DANQUAH, FOUNDER AND PROPRIETOR OF MOSES SCHOOL OF ACCOUNTANCY, KOFORIDUA, GHANA.

AND

THE LATE APOSTLE S. Y. APPIAH, FOUNDER OF THE VOICE OF THE LORD EVANGELICAL CHURCH, GHANA.

TO GOD BE THE GLORY!! AMEN!!

Acknowledgement

ALL Glory and Very Special thanks to JESUS CHRIST my Lord and God who gave me all the wisdom, knowledge, good health and graciously spared me abundant time and life very vital in the production of "PROFESSIONAL INVESTIGATION". All Praise, Glory and Honour be unto Him for ever and ever. Amen.

I wish, also, to acknowledge the strenuous efforts and contribution of Col. John Agyakwa, a Director in the Ghana Army, Burma Camp, Accra; Mr M. K. Gyamfi, retired Deputy Director (Operations) of the Ghana Immigration Service, Accra and Authorhouse Publishers (USA), in making this Book a reality.

Special mention also needs to be made of Mr. Enrico De Simone, Managing Director of De Simone Group Of Companies, Ghana; Mr Tony El Radi of Green Consultancy Ltd, Hohoe, Ghana; Madam Klaudia Elisabeth Raphael (Mrs) and Mr. Detlef Raphael, both resident German expatriates in Ghana; as well as Mr. Bharat Armanani (a.k.a. Mr. Babs) a resident Indian expatriate in Ghana, for the immense encouragement they gave me in the publication of this book. I am forever very much grateful to them.

I cannot do without appreciating the priceless contribution of my wife Madam Cecilia Danquah Selby and our children: Samuel Danquah, an Agricultural Engineer, Tema, Ghana; Evelyn Danquah, student of the University of Cape Coast, Ghana; and Judith Anim-Danquah, Tema, for the immense all-round assistance they offered me in the publication of this Book. I am extremely grateful to them.

I am lastly, but not the least, thankful to Pastor Charles Nartey, Tema, and many others who also made no mean contribution in diverse ways, who are not mentioned here. Their enormous contribution is highly acknowledged.

Many, many thanks to all including my very cherished readers.

E. Anim-Danquah
February, 2018.

INTRODUCTION

Professionalism is key in the conduct of investigation. Wrong arrests, wrong reports, delayed reports, shelving and censuring of vital evidence leading to misleading judgements in prosecution, wrong decision making in policy formulation and so on are very grave concerns in investigation. These have very devastating aftermaths, sooner or later, in the economic and social development of any country; the dire State Security consequences need no elaboration.

The motivation to write PROFESSIONAL INVESTIGATION, and other Investigation Books that I have already published, stemmed from the persistent observation, in my professional practice as an investigator, of many innocent, helpless and poor people convicted wrongfully or remanded without justification. Sometimes truth is not solidly established by investigators; other times, reports are mere fabrication by bogus investigators. In certain instances too the sensational *"quid pro quo"* factor is deployed; a host of other issues culminating in the presentation of wrong reports and hence _false charges_ against innocent and less privileged poor people being painfully convicted and kept behind bars for years are the hallmark of some investigators. There are even certain times when some investigators, for reasons best known to them, are unable to submit any investigation report on suspects and therefore dump them on remand hopelessly for years. God will demand answers to all these brutish acts on the Day of Judgement.

Some of these unfortunate situations are deliberate, calculated and barbaric. In a few cases however, the investigators may not know what to do in certain circumstances and hence just copy blindly from their wicked and greedy colleagues. For instance, it is not a good practice for an investigator to base his charges on just "Statements" obtained from complainants or suspects: whether the statements are properly taken at all remains another matter in itself. These issues are discussed very well in this book.

Now, it is no news to any one that government policies are/should be products of thorough investigations. Policies affect and are meant for the people governed. Therefore before any policy is formulated, the issues calling for such policies must be thoroughly investigated and "Appropriate Reports", including mature assessments, made on all findings before the relevant bodies such as Cabinet draw in to play their roles. Such policies can hardly fail or be rebutted.

But where for political expediency, vicious victimization, and such likes, all borne on the shoulders of personal interests of some influential people or a small group of persons who will just usher themselves into a closet and unleash directives obviously not helpful to those at the receiving end (society), one can be sure of the damning consequences especially to State Security: strikes galore, fire-works across the airwaves and in the print media, etc. Issues like these are discussed in this book.

Modus Operandi, a very important aspect of investigations, is also discussed in detail. It is a very critical tool in the curbing of criminal activities. This Book looks at the critical elements of modus operandi, the factors that influence changes in the modus operandi of criminals and many others. It should be noted here that the main aim of investigations is to solve problems facing society and reform it; merely convicting people and casting them into prison is not the real solution, but the ability to get rid of or reduce the levels of crimes and other misconducts inimical to the building of a healthy society, is what matters most. After all many people have been to prison and come out more lethal criminals than ever.

Another serious and unprofessional issue that is overlooked in certain operational situations is the use of *CONGESTED OFFICES* to conduct interrogation. It is a very unacceptable practice in investigation, if and only if professionalism and excellent results are truly required at any time in investigations. This book also discusses the problem and offers anti-dotes where and when the use of congested offices for investigation is inevitable in prevailing circumstances.

Investigation Reports are not exactly the same as *Interrogation Reports.* A lot of people, including Committees Of Enquiry, often use the latter for the former. The difference between the two Reports is very much expounded in this book. Similarly, *Statements* by themselves also do not constitute investigation reports. '***Professional Investigation***' offers a very clear explanation for that.

The Value Of Information is another critical aspect of investigation, more especially in INTELLIGENCE PRACTICE. Every *useful* information must be RELIABLE, ACCURATE and TIMELY. Proper attention is given to these in the book.

A host of other critical issues in investigations including *Distraction, Evidence, Planning Of Investigations, Interrogation techniques and Effective Report Writing* are equally given a clean treat in this book.

PROFESSIONAL INVESTIGATION is not just an excellent training material for all levels in all **Security Services** and **Intelligence Agencies** but equally a very good source of reference after formal training or during professional practice. For these reasons, very simple language is used throughout. Emphasis is placed on certain words or expressions, as demonstrated in this Introduction. The essence is to ***prompt the reader to take special note of such expressions*** in their respective contexts to enhance his understanding.

Finally, a few hypothetic Study Cases are discussed towards the end of the book to further enhance your reading pleasure.

E. Anim-Danquah
February, 2018, Tema. Ghana.

CONTENTS

CHAPTER 5

CHAPTER 6

CHAPTER 7

CHAPTER 8

CHAPTER 9

CHAPTER 10

CHAPTER 1

BASICS

An interesting event occurred in the early 1980s on a passenger bus travelling from one city to another in a certain country. There were twenty persons on board the vehicle, including the driver. On the way, it occurred to one of the passengers to check his pocket for his money. He did so instantly. Surprisingly, he noticed that five hundred dollars which he kept in his back-pocket was missing. He could not hold it. He sent an alarm. Everybody on the bus was stunned. The driver who was in charge of the vehicle then drove all the passengers to a Police Station where a report was made.

The police, after the necessary formalities, detained two of the passengers who were suspected to have taken the money.

Note that the action or steps initiated by the driver and the Police in this case were both aimed at helping to find out the true facts about where the alleged missing money was so that the owner could have his money back.

This process of *trying* to find out the truth about an allegation, incident, or an uncertainty is what is called ***Investigation.***

In another development, a student left his passport on his desk during a fifteen-minute break after a morning lesson. When break was over and all the students returned to the classroom, he detected that the page which bore a valid U.S. Visa in his passport had been removed. A small peculiar pen which did not belong to him was found on his desk.

He reported the matter to the Class Teacher and gave the teacher the small pen. The teacher in turn did not mention the passport to the class. Rather, he showed the small pen to the class saying that it was found at the Dining Hall and that whoever was or knew the owner could claim it at his or her convenience.

Immediately, two students stood up and mentioned the owner of the pen. They had accompanied the owner of the pen to buy it from a stationery shop in town just the previous day.

A search conducted on the owner of the small pen who belonged to the next classroom, found the missing "Visa Page" of the passport in question on him.

In this example too, the efforts made by the owner of the Passport as well as the teacher in respect of the missing "Visa Page" were all aimed at **ESTABLISHING EVIDENCE IN RELATION TO THE ALLEGED MISSING VISA PAGE.**

The measures taken in both illustrations above to ESTABLISH EVIDENCE about the respective allegations, suspicions or incidents is all investigation is about. Take note that there would be no investigation unless it is prompted or called for, as seen in the examples above.

However, it is a different thing establishing evidence in a case and not providing same in the Investigation Report; it is another matter also to obtain evidence and shelve part or adulterate it in the investigation Report. These are not professional practice in this specialized field.

It must be noted that Investigation is not limited to past events; it can also be carried out on an on-going event or one that is likely to occur in future. The last two are normally conducted using *clandestine principles and expertise* to achieve the required results. The two examples seen so far both concern investigation of past events. *Rumours* are typical instances that can be subjected to clandestine investigations.

Investigation is conducted in every aspect of human life. It is a dynamic and very interesting activity. It takes place in different forms depending on the specific field of human activity that is involved, e.g. Medical,

Audit, Criminal, Immigration, Customs, Fire, Accounting, Architecture, etc. Each of them requires appropriate expertise to handle efficiently and effectively.

TYPES AND FORMS OF INVESTIGATION

Types Of Investigation
An investigation may either be;

    (a)Open   or   (b) *Secret*

The practical use of each of these depends on the circumstances of a particular investigation. Both types can as well be combined in an exercise where and when necessary. They both have their specific characteristics.

Open Investigation

As the name implies, *Open Investigations* are not concealed. All the parties concerned are fully made aware that they are involved in an investigation or an investigation is going on around them.

This type of investigation is more widely used and hence more common than the Secret one. It is usually used for Crimes, Offences, Incidents or Events that have already occurred. Take note, however, that even in an Open Investigation Secret Investigation can also be employed in order to access specific information that are vital to an investigation but not too easy to come by. It all depends on the discretion and strategy of the investigator in a particular situation as well as the nature of the specific task or case on hand.

Secret Investigation

This type of investigation involves the use of technical aids and various forms of clandestine manoeuvres. It is mostly used in 'complex' investigations and intelligence practice. This book does not discuss this type of investigation for National Security reasons. Nevertheless, let us throw a little light on the subject. Secret Investigation is mainly a Covert Activity mostly used for events that are:

(a) About to take place (certain);

(b) Likely to take place (uncertain);

(c) Still going on (certain).

It may also be employed for sensitive events that have already occurred. These may involve issues such as Coup plots, Bank Robberies, Serial Killings, Kidnaping, Cyber Fraud, Sensitive Chieftaincy Disputes and other forms of organized crime. It is also used in the Financial Sector to monitor the abuse of office, non-performance of Contractors, etc.

We shall just limit ourselves to a few characteristics of this subject area in contrast with 'Open Investigation'.

Characteristics of Secret Investigation

This involves:

a. *Surveillance*: this is the secret watching of a person(s),place(s), Organizations(s) Installation(s), or even a whole State in order to obtain useful information about it/them, as the case may be.
b. *Secret Search*: this has to do mainly with the clandestine intrusion into one's premises, e.g. House, Office, Vehicle, Mails, Personal effects, etc. There are specific guiding principles here, but, basically you ensure that you do not leave any trace/mark that could create the least suspicion for any intrusion. Secret Search is carried out at a very high Operational Speed.
c. *Secret Recording* : this includes bugging of telecommunication equipment, secret photography and various other clandestine recordings.
d. *Secret Examination Of Documents*: here, we ensure that we do not leave any trace or mark any where.
e. The person(s), Organization(s), etc. being investigated is/are *not made aware* of the investigation.

f. *No interrogation* takes place. But, elicitation could be employed for the acquisition of specific information.

g. *No Statement* is taken until the main Secret Investigation is over and it becomes necessary to take Statements from certain individuals of special interest to the specific investigation.

h. *Very High Operational Risk*: the risk involved here is very high and hence require much circumspection. Only expert hands are usually employed to direct such exercises.

The purpose of Secret Investigation is mainly to prevent Crime occurrence, to establish the Modus Operandi of sensitive crimes or other events, especially those of interest to State Security and also to obtain direct evidence.

Characteristics of Open Investigation

(a) It is mainly used for events or crimes that have already occurred, e.g. Bank Robberies, Jail Breaks, Unsuccessful Coup d'etats, Fraud, etc.

(b) The person or Organization etc being investigated is ***formally made aware*** of the investigation;

(c) The person or Organization etc being investigated is also ***made aware of the specific offence*** for which the investigation is being conducted;

(d) It can involve formal search (with or without warrant, as the case may be);

(e) Interrogation is involved;

(f) Secret Investigation procedures could/might be employed to support or enhance Open Investigation BUT not vice versa.

Let us consider the following illustration:

On 30th June, 1903, The Police Chief of an European Country received an urgent message from an informant. It read: "MAJOR GEN ALMOND APPLES, COMMANDER OF 2ND INFANTRY BRIGADE OF THE ARMY LEADING A GROUP OF YOUNG MILITARY OFFICERS AND MEN DRAWN FROM THE ARMY, AIRFORCE AND NAVY, REPORTED TO BE HOLDING PRIVATE MEETINGS IN A THICKET ABOUT 2.5KM EAST OF THE JUNGLE WARFARE BASE IN THE CENTRAL PROVINCE. THEY ARE PLOTTING TO OVERTHROW THE GOVERNMENT IN THE NEXT FEW DAYS".

Now, in this hypothesis, we notice that the people are ***IN THE PROCESS OF PLOTTING*** to overthrow the government. So, ***Secret Investigation*** would first have to be used to establish the truth, or otherwise, of the report or allegation and possibly to obtain further evidence for the purpose of either arranging strategies to ***prevent*** the Coup d 'tat or ***arrest*** the identified suspects or both, where necessary. At least some Prima Facie Evidence must be obtained to (a) *confirm or deny the information and/or (b) serve as basis for any appropriate action on it where necessary.*

Granted that some suspects are successfully arrested, then ***Open Investigation*** could be conducted as well (including interrogation) at the appropriate time.

From the *point of suspects' arrest, they are made aware of why they have been arrested,* as required by law. The investigation from that point then becomes an OPEN one because the suspects have been ***formally made aware*** that they are being investigated. Prior to their arrest, ***they were not made aware*** that they were being investigated, and that is the nature of Secret Investigation.

Note that they COULD BE AWARE on their own, or by themselves, that they might be under some sort of Secret Monitoring or investigation. But, the important point is that ***they were not formally made aware*** of any such investigation on them until after their arrest.

Consider the following report also:

"Four security officers have been sentenced to a total of 80 years' imprisonment with hard labour for their various roles in the smuggling of cowpeas along the western frontiers of certain State.

*These, who were picked up four years ago alongside six others, are to serve 20 years each in prison. The Fast Track High Court, presided over by Justice JORHJ JONNES, upheld the case of the prosecution and said **the prosecution was able to lead evidence TO PROVE THE OFFENCES of abetment of unlawful exportation of cowpeas and corruption of a public officer...**"*

The facts of the case were that in December, 1905, the National Cowpeas Board, unhappy with the extent of cowpea smuggling across the borders of the country, employed the services of a special agency to conduct investigation into the activities of State Security Agencies posted along the various border posts of its western frontiers.

Personnel of the contracted special agency carried out the investigations within two years. The team, in the course of the investigations, visited a number of border posts, including Hillsdorf, Kweiksu, Saku, Abrantie Fie and came across a number of security personnel, including the convicts manning the border posts.

As part of their investigations, members of the team presented themselves as ordinary smugglers seeking to smuggle cowpeas to her neighbour to the west. According to the prosecution, the convicts, in their capacity as security personnel, played diverse roles in assisting and facilitating the team to smuggle several bags of cowpea to that sister country.

*In the process, they took huge fees for allowing the **undercover investigating team** to smuggle the commodity to that country. Interactions by the undercover team with the public officials were **captured by hidden cameras.***

__Based on the recordings, FURTHER INVESTIGATIONS were__
__conducted by the Police resulting in the arrest of the convicts." (All__
emphases mine).

You will notice from the facts of this case as published in the Daily that
the nature of the investigation was such that **Secret Investigation** was
inevitable. You will also notice the use of <u>secret cameras</u> to record evidence
(direct evidence) and the use of appropriate **_cover_** right from the onset to
conceal the investigations.

The *Secret Camera* recordings of the activities of the security officers paved
the way for "FURTHER INVESTIGATIONS". Further Investigations
here does not mean a rush into Open Investigation. Rather, further
CLANDESTINE MEASURES were adopted by The Police, in view of
the nature of the task, up to the point of ARRESTS.

The moment an arrest is made the investigation becomes an *Open one*, to
a large extent.

The Private Investigators COULD ONLY USE SECRET
INVESTIGATION, while thereafter the Police combined both Secret
and Open Investigations very well resulting in the arrest and conviction
of the affected security officers.

In this piece, we notice further that:

(a) Secret Investigation was mainly used, especially right from the
onset. Only very few people, who needed to know, actually knew
what was in store.

(b) After Secret Investigation was applied up to some point and
some suspects were picked up by the Police, Open Investigation,
automatically, was roped in and that enabled the suspects to, for
instance, be interrogated and Statements obtained from them.

(c) The exercise was a very good combination of Secret and Open Investigations. Neither of these two types of investigation could have completely helped the situation.

So, you can see the difference between Secret Investigation and Open Investigation in this brief illustration and how effective and interesting a combination of both can be, ***if and only if properly planned and executed.***

FORMS OF INVESTIGATION

Investigations take many forms, depending on what is at stake. We can talk of Medical Investigations, Ballistic Investigation, Audit Investigations, Criminal Investigations, Architectural Investigations and so on. Each is a specialty of its own. Note, however that sometimes Criminal Investigation encompasses various forms of Investigation depending on what is under investigation at a point in time. That is to say, during Criminal Investigations other forms of investigation can be brought into play.

Sometimes a particular investigation would require a combination of two or more of the various forms of investigation just as we have seen with the two types of investigation.

It must be noted here that where an investigator is not very knowledgeable in a particular field of endeavour, he or she should not hesitate to seek assistance from the appropriate expert, when necessary. Unless this is done, the investigator would not be able to arrive at any good findings and cannot therefore be fair in his report. This is because every form of investigation requires specific professional expertise to unearth the required evidence.

Let us consider this example: "One Madam Apple, a landlady, reported to the Immigration Service of a certain country recently that some eight female foreigners came in as students to rent her four-bedroom self-contained flat.

According to Madam Apple, she had observed the ladies for some time and suspected that they were not students as they claimed. Rather, they were commercial sex workers who also engaged in drug trafficking and the shooting of pornographic films with some male foreign nationals in the said house. She said she could not just eject them because their rent advance had not been exhausted.

For these reasons, according to the landlady, she wanted the Immigration Service to arrest and deport them."

Now, when you carefully study this case, you will notice that both the Immigration Service and the Police have respective roles to play in it. The fact that the case mainly bothers on Immigration and also that it was first reported to the Immigration Service does not mean only the Immigration Service has to deal with it.

Immigration will only determine the Immigration Status of each of the foreigners involved (assuming they were successfully arrested). That is, Immigration would find out whether each of them had a Valid Residence or Visitors' Permit and if even "Yes", whether any of the conditions under which each permit was granted had been broken, and so on. The Police, on its part, would tackle the shooting of pornographic films and drug trafficking. In this way a comprehensive report/findings could be made on the issue.

Let us also consider a situation where "an elderly man took a sumptuous meal and died a few hours later after his admission at a hospital, and there was the need to establish the actual cause of death".

An investigation into this case would not only involve the Police. The expertise of someone in the Medical Field (here, a Pathologist) would certainly be required to prove whether the food was poisoned or whether the person died of some other cause. Until that was done, the Police alone could not ascribe criminal charges against anyone.

So, here again you see that at least two forms of investigation must be conducted before reasonably good findings can be made on the issue at stake and a subsequent good investigation report presented.

IMPORTANCE OF INVESTIGATIONS

The main importance of investigations are:

1. To establish the truth of allegations and/or suspicions;

2. To establish the truth of rumours and/or alarms;

3. A critical tool in research;

4. To assist in assembling relevant facts for policy formulation, especially in governance.

These can however be attained if, AND ONLY IF, investigators are able to diligently LOOK FOR and BRING UP PROOFS, facts or evidence, to help decide effectively and efficiently on issues subject for investigations.

Allegations. An allegation is not the same as a "suspicion". In the two illustrations we just looked at in the introduction to this Chapter, the issues raised were both "suspicions". In each, there was just a "sense of something bad that had happened or was about to happen in an environment or to a person". That is a "suspicion". A suspicion may or may not be premised on a reality. In the theft case that occurred on the public bus cited earlier in this chapter, there was suspicion based on "no reality". Money had "disappeared from a passenger's pocket". No one could tell whether or not that claim was a reality. It could be anything. There were **no immediate clues** to SUSPECT anyone; therefore only an 'open suspicion' could hold, for the mean time, for an unknown criminal. An allegation is 'suspicion directed at a specific person or target'. In the example in question, no specific person on the bus could be JUSTIFIABLY HELD as a suspect there and then for which an allegation could be made against him.

It could even happen that the money was:

1. Picked by "goro-boys" at the lorry station even before boarding that bus; or

2. The money was left on a counter of a restaurant by the owner himself when he went to enjoy some drink or snacks over there long before even going to board that bus; or

3. It could be a deliberate false alarm. There could be many other possible situations that could fit into the 'episode'.

However, in case there was enough grounds to REASONABLY SUSPECT one or two persons, then an allegation could be made against such person or persons. So, in the events that ensued on the bus and at the Police Station, it could be that the 'owner of the missing money' had some good grounds to suspect some passengers, thus he could make an allegation against them.

In the case of the missing valid Visa, A PECULIAR PEN was left on the desk of the owner of the passport containing the missing Visa. The owner of the peculiar pen was known and so he could be "factually suspected" of the crime, unless proven otherwise later. Where and when there was such factual suspicion, certainly an allegation could be made to the Police against the person or persons so suspected for which reason such persons could be held as true suspects for prosecution.

From here, however, the onus would lie on the arresting Officer, Investigator or Prosecutor, to prove the guilt of the "suspect". That could only be done by Investigations.

Now turning to "Rumours" and "Alarms", the exponential threats that these pose to security, whether of individuals or a State, is common knowledge.

Some people hold the view that "there is always a degree of truth in every rumour". That may or may not be true. This is an essence of Investigation;

to establish the truth of rumours or alarms so that one is not compelled to respond inappropriately or immaturely to any rumour.

False alarms are even more treacherous than ordinary rumours. Very swift investigations are required in these situations always to nib them in the bud.

Touching on Research, especially into matters that bother on State Security, one cannot rule out investigations. Right from Economic Sabotage through Labour Activities, National Elections, Media Behaviour, "Politics" to Crimes and many more, no effective research can be made without investigations.

At the end of it all, "Policy Formulation" must stem from "real facts", not half-truths, but real and full truths. Many policies especially of governments have failed, crashed or backfired because of such phenomena.

CHAPTER 2

PLANNING

Planning is inevitable in all aspects of human endeavour, investigation no exception.

The planning of investigation hinges on the content and/or requirement for the specific task on hand at a given time and place. Generally, it takes into account:

1. *CLASSIFICATION*

2. *URGENCY*

3. *TERMS OF REFERENCE (TOR)*

4. *AVAILABLE INFORMATION (Is what provided what is truly and exactly meant for the task?)*

5. *WHAT INFORMATION IS LACKING? (For each given point to be thoroughly investigated, we will need to ask: WHAT, WHO, WHERE, WHEN, WHY, WHOM, WHICH and HOW.*

6. *TYPES OF INVESTIGATION TO USE (Secret, Open or Both)*

7. *ARRESTS (Any need or justification? If yes, what procedure? Availability of Detention Facilities?)*

8. *SEARCH (Secret or Open)*

9. *DETENTION (Availability of Good Facilities)*

10. *PRESERVATION OF EVIDENCE (Good facilities to store exhibits under Standard Temperature and Pressure [STP] as well as maintaining Normal Geometric Conditions.*

11. *INTERROGATION (Degrees Of Interrogation to be used)*

12. *COMMENCEMENT/STRATEGY (Where, how and when to begin the Investigation,)*

13. *MEDIUM OF COMMUNICATION*

14. *SOURCES OF INFORMATION (Access: Direct or Indirect?)*

15. *WITNESSES (Access to useful information, Motivation)*

16. *INDEPENDENT WITNESSES (Motivation)*

17. *INTERPRETERS (Motivation)*

18. *FUNDS AND LOGISTICS (Adequate Funding and Logistics and Judicious Use of same to achieve maximum possible results)*

1. CLASSIFICATION

Classification refers to the level or magnitude of special care that needs to be accorded every single piece of information and exhibit/material provided at any investigation. It enables the determination of how every single aspect of an entire investigation should be handled efficiently and effectively right from the point of receipt of a task through to the submission and preservation of the final report.

Information or Reports may be classified as TOP SECRET, SECRET, RESTRICTED, CONFIDENTIAL or PERSONAL, generally. Each of these is informed by the content of the given material.

Here are a few examples:

MATERIAL 1.

"MEMORANDUM

TO: ADI/ENF
FROM: AICO/ENF
DATE OF INFORMATION: 9/11/2009
DATE OF REPORT: 10/11/2009
SUBJECT: SUSPICIOUS PRESENCE OF TERRORISTS

Twenty (20) able-bodied young men, aged between nineteen (19) and thirty (30) years, have been engaged in para-military manoeuvres in a deep valley close to the North-Eastern frontier of the country. They have been observed by local farmers for the past few weeks in the act. It is not known the exact time and how they surfaced there. They are all light skinned, wear thick black and moderately long beards.

Submitted for your attention and directives, please.
Sgd. (Case Officer)."

A careful look at the content of the above hypothetical source/information report brings into focus its very high security value, even though unconfirmed. It is such that not many hands need to handle it, aside its urgency. One may therefore classify such a report or piece of information as "RESTRICTED" or "SECRET".

MATERIAL 2.

"MEMORANDUM

TO: OIC/CRIME, CRHQ
FROM: STATION OFFICER, MANGOO.
INFO: 2 i/c
DATE: 14/04/1987.

SUBJECT: RE-ALLEGED EXTORTION: ASP SPINER AVOCADO AND D/CPL STREAM GOROB

Please refer to your instructions on the above subject matter.

INTRODUCTION: The matter brought up for investigation was that ASP Spiner Avocado and one other person had allegedly extorted three thousand five hundred US dollars ($3,500) from a foreigner in the capital with the promise to regularize his stay in the country but they failed to deliver on their promise.*

TERMS OF REFERENCE

(i)   *To investigate, thoroughly, the above allegation and submit a report soonest.*

(ii)   *To make any recommendation, where appropriate, for the necessary measures to be taken to effectively and efficiently address the issue, taking into consideration the image of the Service and the Country as a whole.*

SUMMARY OF FINDINGS

1. *ASP Spiner Avocado could not explain how he arrived at the $3,500 (three thousand five hundred US Dollars) penalty against the complainant.*

2. *The complainant last left this country on 25/1/1986, through the Bogus-Z International Airport (BZIA), but there was no evidence on how and when he returned here,*

3. *D/Cpl Stream GOROB, the other alleged accomplice of ASP Spiner AVOCADO, was not found to have played any active role in the transaction.*

INVESTIGATION

ASP Spiner AVOCADO was carefully interrogated on the allegation, in the presence of an Independent Witness on three (3) different occasions: 5/6/1987, 6/6/1987 and 9/6/1987. Each lasted ninety (90) minutes on the average, during which he mentioned D/Cpl Stream GOROB, his official driver, as his "companion" who ran errands for him in the transaction. According to ASP AVOCADO, he formally reported the matter to the Divisional Commander, C/Supt. Greenleaf YELLOWS, who verbally mandated him (ASP AVOCADO) to investigate it.

According to ASP AVOCADO, he and D/CPL GOROB went to the Whiteocean Hotel located towards the eastern gate of the city, on 28/2/1987 at about noon and came across a gentleman who gave his name as Dr ARC.

The investigation established that "Dr. ARC, holder of Passport No. MM8167118 NB, issued on 15/3/1982 in Molasses and due to expire on 14/3/1992, last left this country on 25/1/1986 but there was no indication in his passport showing how, where and when he re-entered this country."

It was established that ASP AVOCADO collected $3,000 (three thousand US dollars) as penalty for "overstay" and a further $500 (five hundred US dollars), processing fee for regularisation of stay from Dr. ARC in his hotel room, No. BX.19, on 29/2/1987 at about 21.30 hours GMT. Both amounts were in cash.

ASP AVOCADO did not deny this claim by Dr. ARC when a confrontation was organized between them during interrogation.

On how ASP AVOCADO managed to calculate the alleged overstay penalty against the complainant (Dr. ARC), ASP AVOCADO had no explanation to offer.

D/CPL Stream GOROB corroborated ASP AVOCADO's assertion that he, GOROB, was not present when the various monies were agreed upon between the complainant and ASP AVOCADO and in the subsequent collection of the $3,500 from Dr. ARC.

COMMENTS

The circumstances surrounding the whole transaction or offence is quite strange on the part of ASP AVOCADO, considering his status.

RECOMMENDATION

In view of the findings of the investigation, the following recommendations are made:

(i)   *ASP AVOCADO be subjected to the provisions of the Standing Orders of the Service and appropriate sanctions applied on him.*

(ii)   *He should additionally be made to refund all the illegally collected monies from the complainant, Dr ARC.*

(iii)   *The complainant, who was found to have entered the country illegally, infringes on the Immigration Laws of the country. He should be processed for Court for the necessary Statutory Orders for his removal from the country to be effected, among other things that the Court may decide.*

(iv)   *D/CPL Stream GOROB was not found to have played any significant role in the offence under investigation. He should be exonerated accordingly.*

Respectfully submitted, please.
Sgd. (Case Officer)."

This is a typical Investigation Report. In its classification, we need to very carefully assess its content. We notice that it involves at least a Senior Officer of the Police Service and for that matter it needs to be handled very carefully so as to protect the image of the Service but not necessarily the reputation of ASP AVOCADO.

At the same time, however, there are not too many issues in that material that call for "Restricted Access", relatively.

We may therefore conveniently classify this report as "Confidential".

This indicates that even though the content of the report does not demand very stern concealment, it somehow cannot also be handled anyhow or recklessly.

URGENCY

Urgency tells how fast we should, or have to work, on a given material. Once again, the content determines the urgency. In most cases, issues that directly affect State Security or human lives require more urgent response, relatively.

In the two Materials cited under 'Classification' earlier, "Material 1" is a terrorist-related report. This has a direct bearing on State Security and will therefore require urgent attention. "Material 2", on the other hand, deals with an ordinary extortion case and unless there is a special order from superior officers for a prompt response, this assignment can go with a "normal touch".

The above explanation is only in relative terms. Every assignment must be given due attention and not unnecessarily delayed in order not to deny justice to anyone, for, "Justice delayed is justice denied", as the saying goes.

TERMS OF REFERENCE

The *Terms Of Reference* (TOR) constitutes the fulcrum for planning an investigation. It spells out the direction a specific investigation or exercise must go and hence an extremely important aspect in the conduct of investigation.

It is therefore very necessary for the investigator to ensure that <u>he knows and understands the TOR very well before setting out to do any planning or carrying out any exercise.</u> In case an investigator is not quite clear about any aspect of the TOR, it is better to quickly seek clarification from appropriate quarters, if possible, than to lean on a wrong idea to do a wrong job and present an unwanted report to discredit himself and possibly his Organisation or Service.

In Material 2 cited under *Classification* earlier, we see specific instructions or directives required of the investigation clearly spelt out by the Assigning Authority. Such operational instructions constitute the TOR for the specific exercise. The investigator is thus required to ensure he covers all the TOR and report as exhaustively as possible.

Now, there are situations where the TOR is not specified. In such instances, the investigator has to think through the content of the given material maturely and determine the TOR himself to guide his investigation. This is an area/situation where and when experience on the job counts.

Consider the following material:

"*Material 3*

Memorandum

Classification: Confidential
To: Station Officer, Camp B4.
From: Director, Special Operations, Hqrs.
Date: 21/09/2013
Subject: Stadium Disaster

A radio station in the capital has just reported hooliganism at the National Sports Stadium during a football match between Bully-Bully SC and Phobophobia FC. Several people are reported dead and many others injured as a result. Grateful investigate. Treat urgent."

In this material, the only instruction given is to "INVESTIGATE"; just that. It will therefore be the responsibility of the investigator to determine the salient areas for thorough investigation since the TOR is not elaborate or specified.

We shall have to determine what is the <u>main focus</u> of such an investigation by ourselves. We may consider, for the TOR, such points as:

(i)   What actually is going on and/or has gone on?

(ii)   What is/was the cause?

(iii)   Any casualties? If yes, what number is involved?, what are their respective identities? What is the nature and degree of injury of each casualty? What is their respective response to treatment? Any deaths? Where is each casualty located?

(iv)   Any arrests made or to be made?

(v)   Any detentions and place of detention

(vi)   Recommendation to prevent any recurrence in future?

Let us take note that even though the directive only said "Investigate", the investigator is obliged to Report on his findings.

Furthermore, the name of the Radio Station may be necessary in the investigation and subsequent Report where and when the information allegedly put on air turns out to be completely false, after visiting the National Sports Stadium to find no trace of any such event as reported. Then, the Radio Station in question will have to be fished out to answer criminal charges for causing fear and panic, raising false alarm and such likes as the Statute Books will prescribe at the time.

Otherwise, the name of the Radio Station may not be too relevant in the investigation so long as the National Stadium where the alleged disaster took place can be located.

AVAILABLE INFORMATION

This refers to the facts contained in an assignment and here, we ask ourselves:

Is the information provided what is truly and exactly meant for the exercise?

Just as in the case of the TOR, the investigator needs to KNOW and UNDERSTAND the content very well since that is going to form the basis for planning the given investigation. The content of the available information must also match the TOR for the specific exercise.

In "Material 3" discussed above, the following information was provided:

(i)   Main event/problem that is a source of worry: *several persons allegedly dead and many injured;*

(ii)   *Place: National Sports Stadium*

From this analysis, one will notice that there are several information gaps to be filled.

MISSING INFORMATION

This is the *crux* of investigation. It is subject to the available information and the TOR. In other words, we can know the information that is lacking, and which the investigation must of course fish out and bring up truthfully and accurately, after a very <u>careful study</u> of the available information, or the initial information provided, and the TOR. Any failure or lapse here can adversely affect the planning and successful conduct of the investigation and hence its execution and subsequent report.

In trying to find out answers to missing information, we normally probe on the premises of: *WHAT, WHO, WHERE, WHEN, WHOM, WHICH, WHY and HOW {7 Ws and 1 H}* for each point raised in the initial or raw information provided, always <u>paying particular attention</u> at the same time to the TOR; i.e.

(i)   WHAT has happened, is happening or is about to happen?

(ii)   WHO did, is doing or intends to do what?

(iii)   WHERE did that happen, is that happening or is about to happen?

(iv)   WHEN did that happen, is that happening or is about to happen?

(v)   WHOM was the act directed at, is being directed at or is about to be directed at?

Or suffer from the act?

(i)   WHICH of the lot <u>specifically did what or suffered what?</u>

(ii)   WHY did that happen, or is that happening or about to happen? i.e for what reason?

(iii)   HOW did the act happen, or is it happening or about to happen?

For convenience sake, let us reproduce the main text for Material 3 for this discussion.

"…A radio station in the capital has just reported hooliganism at the National Sports Stadium. Several people are reported dead and many others injured. Grateful investigate. …Urgent."

As seen earlier, we know from the initial information (raw information) that:

1.   There was an alleged hooliganism;

2.   The event allegedly occurred at the National Sports Stadium;

3.   Several people have allegedly lost their lives and others injured.

These are the three main given facts provided for the investigation. The name of the radio station was not specified.

Let us take the first item, <u>granted that what was reported actually took place as indicated.</u> That is "hooliganism". For this alone, we can ask questions like:

<u>WHAT specifically happened? And WHAT was the cause?</u> Was is throwing of stones, broken bottles, sachet bags of water, clubs, breaking and throwing of stadium chairs, use of firearms into the crowd, etc.

If we know WHAT exactly happened, then we shall need to know WHO did what? WHO were throwing the missiles? If we know who did what, then we come to WHERE and WHEN did that happen; perhaps the event was limited to the Popular Stands, Western Wing, Press Section or the VIP Stand, or outside the Stadium; who knows. <u>Note that we deal with specifics when it comes to investigation.</u>

On the question of WHEN, we may ask <u>what time of day </u>the event occurred and on what

date? From here we look at <u>WHY all that disturbance at that time?</u> What reason led to the disturbance?

Literally, when we consider the renowned scientist Sir Isaac Newton's Laws on Motion which state, inter alia, that :

(a) *A system will remain at rest or in uniform motion unless it is acted upon by an external force; and*

(b) *Action and reaction are equal and opposite,*

then, if nothing untoward happened, the serenity or sanity in the atmosphere at the National Sports Stadium at the very time could not be disturbed. Definitely something must have triggered the whole episode.

In effect, many people will react the same manner they are affected by the actions of their provocateurs, especially in the environment of a Sports Stadium where and when a live football match was taking place, hence the hooliganism.

So then, **what was the actual cause?** Was is the case of an off-side goal that was allowed by the referee or that a strange penalty was awarded on the brink of full time to give undue advantage to one side? Was the event just a spontaneous one or it was pre-meditated, planned and executed to achieve a specific objective? If pre-meditated and planned, when, where, why and by who? Was it <u>long before the match, just before the match</u> <u>or during the match, etc.? These, and similar questions, all have their</u> <u>respective implications.</u>

The issue of WHOM also comes in. It refers to WHO SUFFERS OR SUFFERED WHAT? That is, who was/were at the receiving end of the hooliganism? Any victims? What are their specific identities? Any damage caused to any installation or other facility? Are any still on admission at the hospital? Who are they and at which hospital are they admitted? Who were treated and discharged, and so on.

The question of WHICH, on its part, seeks to <u>DISTINGUISH </u>between situations, items or persons <u>collectively involved </u>or <u>affected</u> in an occurrence, among others, for specific reasons.

For this question on hooliganism, we may ask: *WHICH of the actors were* *throwing stones and which were firing weapons or breaking stadium chairs* *and throwing same into the crowd; which of them broke the Stadium Gate.* *Certainly individuals among the crowd did not all perform the same activity -* *some did not even take part at all but fled for their safety. Maybe those wearing* *yellow shirts, being supporters of BULLY-BULLY SC were those found to be* *throwing stones and sticks while those wearing red shirts were those found* *breaking Stadium Chairs and hurling bags of sachet water into the crowds,* *the latter being followers of PHOBOPHOBIA FC and so on.*

In respect of victims too, we shall have to find out WHICH of them were children, females or males and their respective age distribution.

Which of them were match officials, top government officials, Members of Parliament, press men, football players, etc.

So, the pronoun 'WHICH' is used in investigation to distinguish between the elements of specific findings for clarity purposes.

Then comes the big question of HOW? This explains the <u>manner</u> the alleged event (here hooliganism) took place. Was it violent? Were war songs chanted by any group? Etc.

We are also told "the event took place at the National Sports Stadium". We shall have to ask: Did any event take place at all at the given time and day/date? WHAT event? WHO provided security there, whether or not there was any event there? HOW many of them? WHAT was their composition? WHAT was the proportion of males to females on this security team? WHAT damage was caused to the structure of the Stadium? WHICH items were destroyed? WHICH parts suffered the most damage? and so on.

We are again told: "several people have allegedly lost their lives and others injured". This aspect has been taken care of in the explanation given under "hooliganism" above.

If we are presenting a full-scale Report, formally, we shall have to do the same for the other two items too, and even more, and we shall be surprised at the volume of concrete facts we shall have in our Report. This is one reason why planning is very important in investigations.

It will make your work relatively less cumbersome.

TYPE OF INVESTIGATION TO USE

This is another critical aspect of the planning process. Any slip here can very much endanger the whole exercise given.

As we saw earlier in this book, there are two types of investigation: Secret Investigation and Open Investigation. The choice of any of these, or a combination of both, for any investigation is subject to the content or requirement of the specific case.

Let us bring up "MATERIAL 1" for this discussion.

"...An unconfirmed source report indicates that a group of young energetic men numbering about twenty (20), aged between 20years and 30years, have been engaged in para-military manoeuvres in a deep valley close to the North-Eastern frontier of the country. They have been observed by local farmers for the past few weeks in the act. It is not however known, the exact time and how they surfaced there. They are all light-skinned and mostly wear thick black moustaches matched with moderately long beards."

This is just a piece of very raw information provided. No specific TOR has been provided yet. Supposing such information were directed to you as a Commanding Officer, what type of investigation would be recommended for the establishment of the facts of this unconfirmed source report?

When we consider the content well, we may first classify the report as "Secret or Restricted". This immediately reminds us to be very cautious with the content and every single step we may want to adopt to delve into the issues raised therein.

This in turn suggests the use of "Clandestine Methods" or "Secret Investigation", mainly, to establish the required facts. We may, among other things, consider or try to establish:

(i)   Whether or not there is any such para-military manoeuvres anywhere in the area mentioned (or possibly in any other part of the entire country).

(ii)   If yes, how many people are involved, and from where have they moved in?; what was their respective points of entry into the country?; what is their age bracket?

(iii)   What are their likely, or certain (if possible), identities including nationalities?

(iv)   Who is their host and what is host's motivation/relationship with the group?

(v)   Any knowledge about the trainers?

(vi)   What type of training facilities, or weapons, are in use there?

(vii)   How long does each training session last, (in estimation)?

(viii)   What are the days and time of training (deep night, dawn, afternoon etc).

(ix)   The exact identity of the unusual location where they are reportedly based and whose property that is; ("...IN A DEEP VALLEY CLOSE TO THE NORTH-EASTERN BORDER).

(x)   The type/nature of exercises they are allegedly engaged in ("para-military").

(xi)   Why they chose to pitch camp "In a deep valley" and "close to a frontier"?

(xii)   WHEN and HOW they ARRIVED or SETTLED in the area - by what means?

(xiii)   Do they hibernate? If yes, how?

(xiv)   WHAT is the nature of security around them : as individuals, as a group, training grounds, etc?

Issues of such nature quickly raise eye-brows and call for extra care. Clandestine means must certainly be applied to first confirm the above facts. Besides, if positive, there *may* be the need also to round up all the suspects for interrogation. This requires that none of them should be alerted in any wise prior to and during the confirmation of the facts of the Report and their subsequent arrests, granted that truly some persons are camping in the given location, or even any other part of the country in the same or similar circumstance.

Such an exercise must be a clandestine one, at least because of :

(i)   Its sensitive nature (if and only if the Report is factual);

(ii)   The risks/dangers involved, both to the individual investigators and the State;

(iii)   If the suspects detect they are being monitored by Security Agents and they <u>disappear</u> from the area, they are likely to re-strategize and hence become more dangerous to State Security than before.

Now, should this critical initial part of the investigation be successful, and some arrest(s) effected, then the exercise becomes somewhat an OPEN one. Open Investigation can then be roped in, for instance when it comes to interrogation of the suspects so arrested.

Prior to any arrests, <u>Secret Search</u> could be conducted on any of them for material evidence, <u>but only where and when possible.</u> After any arrests made, both Secret and Open Searches could be used on any of them for evidence.

So in effect, and even without getting into too much details, we see clearly that both Open and Secret Investigation can be combined in an exercise depending on its content and requirement.

INTERROGATION

Here we consider among other things:

(i)   The type or degree of interrogation to employ for each suspect: 1st, 2nd or 3rd Degree.

(ii) Where, When and How to begin the interrogation. It is for instance very important to determine the order of interrogation, i.e. who should be interrogated first, who next and so on (See the Chapter on Interrogation).

(iii) The medium of communication (language to be used for the interrogation: sign language, French, or what, and the proficiency of the assigned interrogators in them).

(iv) The availability of a reliable Independent Witness and his motivation;

(v) The availability of a reliable Interpreter and his motivation;

(vi) Possible distractions

among others, and quickly make the necessary arrangements to meet these requirements, where and when necessary.

MOTIVATION

The level of access to reliable information quite often depends on "Motivation" of human sources of information. Such motivation may be Political, Patriotism, Monetary, Self-Interest, Social/Academic Belonging, and so on. This must very carefully be discerned by the investigator in making the appropriate choices of persons to assist in his work. In case of a mistake, the other side of the coin may not be too helpful or pleasant.

ACCESS TO USEFUL INFORMATION

Investigation ordinarily seeks to *confirm* or *deny* any given information and also *establish* the required unknown. In doing this, we shall have to consider very carefully "THE SOURCES OF INFORMATION" and ask ourselves: what level of ACCESS (direct or indirect) is/are available to us, how RELIABLE, TIMELY and ACCURATE will such information from various sources prove to be. Such sources include Suspects, Witnesses, Informants, Crime Scene, Publications, Bills, and so on, depending on the type of investigation on hand.

INDEPENDENT WITNESSES

The use of Independent Witnesses in investigations, notably during interrogation and writing of Statements, is extremely important. Yet, many investigators overlook it to their own detriment. We need to make special mention of where and when a suspect has to be Cautioned; that is, taking Cautioned Statements. (See the chapter on Interrogation or Statements).

INTERPRETERS

Will there be any need at all for an Interpreter or Interpreters or do we anticipate any language difficulties? If yes, then we can arrange very swiftly for one or more depending on the diversity of languages that will be used in the investigation.

These solve the problem of communication or language gaps between the investigators and subject of interrogation (suspects, accused, witnesses, etc). As mentioned earlier, they must be very carefully selected by the investigators for purposes of an efficient job done including the security of the exercise itself, among others.

INFORMATION GATHERING *(See 'Sources Of Information')*

Information gathering in investigation is a very meticulous activity. It requires much tact and resilience. It must be timely since information tends to lose value with time.

Information gathering may involve Interrogation, Elicitation, Visit to the Crime Scene, Interviews, Surveillance, Search, among others and is of course subject to the nature of the assignment given.

NEED FOR PROFESSIONAL/TECHNICAL ASSISTANCE

When conducting investigation into issues bothering on specialties that the investigators may not be very conversant with, it is always advisable to seek _very reliable expert hands in that field_ in order to obtain better results. Supposing Police Investigators were conducting investigation into a case that had to do with say Architecture, Ballistics or Commerce, unless any of the Police Investigators in question was a professional in the specific area, the assistance of a RELIABLE PROFESSIONAL must be sought and swiftly too. That is so because every profession has its own technicalities, including technical language (language register). Investigators risk (a) being unable to ask appropriate questions (b) being confused by suspects in their answers to interrogators' inquisition and (c) being outwitted by smart suspects, if they refuse or fail to seek the necessary technical assistance, when required.

ANTICIPATION OF POSSIBLE INFLUENCES

We also need to anticipate possible difficulties or obstructions and determine how to circumvent them smoothly (not rudely or abrasively; we must think about the future). Instances include unnecessary interference and sometimes even threats from interested parties such as, past school mates, family relations, traditional authorities, colleague investigators, our own direct bosses, our former bosses, etc, when any of these has personal interest in a case and would want to use every means to direct the way a case must go.

But, as a professional requirement, the investigator confronted with such a problem just needs to be nice with such personalities, ensuring that he avoids making any promise whatsoever, and then reporting only the truth. The same people will hail you in future for doing the right thing by keeping to the truth, if only they are responsible enough. If you do otherwise, the same people will sit somewhere and slam you.

REPORTS

Here all evidence must be presented fully, accurately, factually and timely. Half truths or compromised truths must be avoided always.

Findings should be presented very clearly, concisely and in a very orderly manner. All references, including Attachments, should be very <u>clear and accurate</u>. We must ensure that our Report flows smoothly to its logical end such that one may even want to enjoy reading it over and over again. Investigation Reports should not be delayed.

We shall have to ensure that all names are presented in full and in their CORRECT SPELLING. We should note that KWESI AFRANE, KWESI AFRANIE, KWASI AFRANE, for instance, do not mean the same person legally, even though have the same pronunciation. Always check the correct spelling of names very carefully before using them in any Investigation Report. Names can be very strong issues of contention in Court. A better thing to do is to always give a person under investigation scribbling materials to pen down his own FULL NAME; (ensure to keep that piece of paper or note book very well for future reference). But, where the suspect or witness cannot write himself, he can spell his name out for the investigator to write it down, and still it is better for the Independent Witness to take up this task. (See the Chapter on Report Writing).

INTERIM REPORTS

Sometimes because of the urgency of an exercise, we may need to submit an Interim Report within the shortest possible time; it could be the same day the request was handed in or a few days later.

Policy makers, for instance, may need to take an urgent decision on say an imminent strike action by Medical Doctors in less than 24 hours and which can have a very devastating impact on the citizenry as well as the international community and hence against the government. It may also involve other issues like espionage, terrorism or a suspicious troop movement that can threaten the Security of the State and for which **very urgent steps must be taken to save the situation.** In situations like this, Interim Reports are submitted quickly first. Usually, Interim Reports are premised on Prima Facie and Circumstantial pieces of Evidence, it should be noted, and could be rebutted.

Sadly, some investigators present Interim Reports and that ends it all. That is a very bad practice which must always be discouraged, irrespective of the nature of the investigation. (See the Chapter on Report Writing).

NOTE: Do not forget to keep an accurate Diary Of Action any time you are carrying out an investigation. It helps a lot in various ways, especially when it comes to Report Writing.

AVAILABILITY OF FUNDS/LOGISTICS

It is essential for investigators to ensure, in all investigations, the availability of adequate FUNDING and LOGISTICS and a VERY JUDICIOUS USE OF SAME. In other words, how much can reasonably take care of the entire investigation such that we shall not be coming for more money every now and then. Cumbersome bureaucratic procedures in securing funding for an exercise can cause dangerous delays which, in turn, can adversely affect any investigation. At the same time, there should always be a judicious use of funds provided for investigation. A contrary position, on the part of investigators, can also effectively constrict an exercise and hence defeat its ultimate objective. Furthermore, we shall need to determine the logistical requirement for an exercise. These include good vehicles as well as relevant technical aids. Note that only relevant technical aids are referred to here, and not an unnecessary flamboyant display of gadgets for the fun of it. If not available, how quickly can they be obtained for the exercise? Statement Forms and Bail Forms should always be in abundance in criminal investigations.

CHAPTER 3

EVIDENCE

The main focus of every investigation is *Evidence*. The investigator must be able to **obtain** and **provide sufficient proof** to either **confirm** or **deny** an allegation, suspicion or other issues (*Research*) under investigation.

But before this can be done, the investigator or Case Officer must **know** and **understand** very well the **Specific Requirements** of the specific investigation.

It must be noted very carefully, to begin with, that every investigation can affect someone's life or future in a way. The investigator or Case Officer must therefore not entertain any prejudice. He must guard against hearsays as well as fabrication and influences from various quarters such as close relations, higher authority, moral considerations, etc. These have a very high potential of defeating the purpose of an investigation. Proper planning of work, timely and accurate reporting and very good preservation of information obtained during investigation are inevitable components of investigation.

Having understood these things, let us now proceed to look at **EVIDENCE**, the main focus of every investigation.

EVIDENCE is every available information that tends to prove the existence or non-existence of a fact.

Kinds of Evidence

There are two main kinds of evidence. These are;

(a) Direct Evidence and

(b) Circumstantial Evidence.

Direct Evidence

Direct Evidence is <u>every available information</u> that tends to prove or disprove the existence or non-existence of an issue obtained by *<u>direct observation or recording</u>*, e.g. a picture taken at the time an event takes place or an eye-witness account. In both cases you notice that there is a *<u>personal and direct knowledge</u>* of the event or "required facts" by the photographer or the eye witness. Such is the best form of direct evidence.

Consider this scenario: "A carpenter and his apprentice stood on the roof of a two-storey building one hot afternoon working. They both had a very clear view of the compound of a small bungalow about 100metres away. They spotted two young men, one of whom the apprentice schooled with and knew very well. These two guys were seen testing the padlock on the main gate to that bungalow with different keys successively until they eventually gained access to the bungalow. They went straight to a new blue-black Mercedez Benz car parked at the bungalow, entered it with cheeky ease and drove off. The carpenter and his apprentice suspected foul play and therefore quickly raised an alarm but that could not help matters. The thieves were gone. The carpenter lodged a complaint with the nearest Police Station, located about 800metres away. The apprentice carpenter gave the necessary information on his classmate 'suspect' to the Police who acted very swiftly and professionally on the information. By 6 a.m. the following day, both robbers were in Police grips and the stolen car impounded and safely parked at the Police Station."

In the investigation of this case, the main witnesses were the carpenter and his apprentice. They were the only known persons who **saw** the entire robbery **directly.** The evidence that would be provided by the carpenter and his apprentice, as eye witnesses, would be Direct Evidence. Both were within range to actually have adequate view of the robbery; visibility was also good on a hot afternoon. (Some people will twist direct evidence or even shelve it for flimsy reasons best known to them. This is very bad.)

Circumstantial Evidence:

This refers to information that proves facts which support the main fact in dispute, but such information or Evidence *does not directly or sufficiently* prove the main fact by itself.

For instance, a witness gave Circumstantial Evidence in a case that he "saw suspect Mr. Mango BLACKSHOE coming from the house where fake dollars were being printed". That alone **does not necessarily prove** that suspect Mr. BLACKSHOE actually mints fake dollars. *It could be that Mr. BLACKSHOE is involved but the available information is not strong enough to hold him guilty. This is what is called CIRCUMSTANTIAL EVIDENCE. His situation* **ONLY** *suggests a likelihood of involvement but not a concrete proof or fact.* Supposing the witness said he saw Murphy Jackson printing fake dollars in the said house, that certainly is a different matter altogether. In that instance, Murphy Jackson was caught in the act of printing fake dollars. Such piece is "Direct Evidence".

Furthermore, granted that a witness reported "seeing a woman or man coming from a man's /woman's room (as the case may be) deep night or at dawn. This can **only suggest** a sexual activity between them that night or dawn, **but it does not necessarily prove** such suspicion or allegation. They can be blood relations, who knows. There can be several morally sound reasons.

If real proof becomes necessary, then an *Opinion Evidence* will have to be sought immediately from Medical Experts on the two. The proof of "sexual engagement" by Medical Experts here, even though can be admissible as Direct Evidence, will still draw strength from the *Presumption* that "public officers have properly discharged their duties".

Note that in these two cases, the suspects "were **_not_** found **_directly_** committing any crime". Rather, each of them was only found **_coming from the area_** where the respective offences were supposedly committed.

That can only "suggest" that each of the suspects **_could have taken part_** in the respective crimes. This is Circumstantial Evidence - evidence based on circumstances. It only points to a **possibility** and **not a fact for sure or a certainty.**

BURDEN OF PROOF

Even though The *Burden Of Proof* normally comes in during a trial, the investigator however needs to have an idea about it in order to be familiar with the situation in the Law Courts. A knowledge of the Burden Of Proof, in respect of each investigation, can help the investigator when it comes to "*Observation, Comments or Recommendation*" in his Final Report. It pays in the analyses of Reports.

The investigator needs to have an idea about **who** must provide **what** evidence, or proof, in any particular case, even though he cannot compel such evidence. He must know **who has the obligation to prove** that an issue under investigation is true or not.

During an investigation it is required that **_sufficient convincing evidence_** should be *obtained* and *provided* by the investigator. The duty of providing such evidence or information is called the BURDEN OF PROOF. It is an **obligation to provide evidence** to prove or disprove a piece of information in contention.

In criminal cases, this obligation lies on the investigator, or the prosecution. In civil cases, the Burden of Proof lies on the person making the case, normally called the "Plaintiff' or "Applicant". In other words, "he who alleges must prove his case beyond reasonable doubts."

Let's look at this: "On 2nd January, 2009, while checking in for a flight at the Bale International Airport, [BIA], Mr. EXXE was arrested by officials of the Narcotics Control Board [NACOB] on suspicion of carrying narcotic drugs. During a search, eighty (80) kilogrammes of cocaine was found on him at the BIA."

Now, in this example, the onus lies on the **the arresting authority** [NACOB] to prove beyond reasonable doubts that YES INDEED MR. EXXE HAS COMMITTED THE OFFENCE. In other words, the Burden of Proof in this matter lies on the NACOB officials and not Mr. EXXE, the suspect. The NACOB Officer who arrested Mr. EXXE must prove beyond reasonable doubts that he indeed found that whole quantity of the specific narcotic drug on Mr. EXXE at the given place and time.

Again, if a Police Officer arrests a pick-pocket at a marketplace, for instance, it is up to that Police Officer who effected the arrest to prove that indeed that suspect is culpable. We thus say the Burden of Proof lies on the Police to prove the 'offence' they are holding the pick-pocket for, beyond reasonable doubts. Take note: these are all for Criminal Cases, not civil.

On the other hand, if some land guards go to seize a parcel of land at Baatsonaa, belonging to Mr.BECEY, for instance, in contesting such a case before the law, it will be up to the land guards to prove the true owner of that parcel of land in contention, else they cannot lay any claim to it. It does not matter whether Mr. BECEY is the true owner of the land he is occupying or not. The land guards who are laying claim to the land must prove beyond reasonable doubts that they truly own the land (or their clients). The Burden of Proof will lie on the land guards. This is for Civil Cases.

In some immigration offences, which are equally criminal however, the Burden of Proof lies on the suspect or accused. For instance, Section 8 (2) of the Immigration Laws of a certain country provides that "A person who enters that country while he is a prohibited immigrant commits an offence..." Section 8 (3) of this Act specifically provides that "**the Burden of Proof...lies upon that person**" found or suspected to have fallen foul of that law. If Mr. QUINTOXIN steals his way into that country and the local security network picks him up, it will be his own responsibility to prove beyond reasonable doubts that his presence in Ghana is legal at the time of his arrest, else he goes in for the 'cool house'. The Burden of Proof lies squarely on him.

ADMISSIBLE AND INADMISSIBLE EVIDENCE

It is very important for an investigator to know the **value** of every piece of information at his disposal in the course of investigation. An Investigator must therefore always ensure that the evidence he is obtaining or submitting in his Report can be Admissible in court; that it can really stand the test of time. This is a very important aspect of investigation that calls for special emphasis. It is the practice of some investigators to deliberately leave out the most important evidence in their Reports in order to weaken the case, altogether, for one side of the investigation due to personal interests or other influences. Others too do not take pains to do the work well; some too are just naïve, and both are unable to bring out the needed information or evidence from suspects, accused or witnesses. Many unfair prosecutions as well as numerous and, in some cases, unnecessary adjournment of very simple and straightforward cases in the Law Courts, can be attributed to some of these things.

Whatever the circumstance, a professional investigator must acknowledge the simple fact that his main duty in every investigation is to **obtain Admissible Evidence and present same (not half truths) in his Report.** That is the mark of a professional in this field. This can save his own reputation in public, especially should the case come up for hearing in Court.

Generally, in order to be admissible, Evidence must:-

(i)   be relevant to the issues at stake,

(ii)   be competent under established rules of law and

(iii)   be material in the sense of having some reasonable tendency to prove or disprove issues under investigation or before court. That is, has it got the real substance, under existing Laws and Regulations, to prove or disprove a case in contention? The investigator needs to constantly weigh his evidence, obtained in the course of his work, against these three pillars, especially before bringing them up in his Report.

Admissible Evidence is mostly Direct, and Oral Evidence is an example. Oral Evidence must generally be based on the **direct observation** of the person providing such evidence. In some cases, however, the admissibility of evidence depends on certain conditions. For instance:

i.　***Circumstantial Evidence*** is admissible only in certain situations. Such evidence, instead of tending directly to prove or disprove the fact of a case, rather relates to other facts which common knowledge and experience have probably closely associated with the facts of the case.

ii.　***Hearsay Evidence*** is also not admissible but has exceptions. e.g. dying declarations, declarations about family history, reputation, official records, spontaneous exclamations, statements of persons naturally disabled, etc. Hearsay Evidence is that which is not based on the direct personal observation of the one providing such evidence. It is not a first-hand information. The one providing such evidence says "he heard others say..." rather than what he personally knows from first-hand experience.

iii.　***Opinion Evidence***, like hearsay evidence, is not admissible but has exceptions as well. That is, experts or very skilled persons may be called upon to express opinions on issues which fall within their fields of specialization, e.g. A Medical Doctor may be called upon to express his opinion or to testify as to the probable nature/cause of a particular injury - whether it was inflicted by a cutlass, bullet, physical blow, fire, motor accident, etc.

Generally, however, witnesses are not usually allowed to express their opinions, inferences, impressions and conclusions since to do so would result in an invasion of the province of the investigator or jury; (See Report Writing). They are only required to provide all evidence at their disposal in any given case where their cooperation is needed.

Remember that an opinion is just an individual belief, estimation or judgement about somebody or something, which is not necessarily based on fact or knowledge.

iv.   ***Presumptions:*** If Evidence about a fact or issue is lacking, a rule of law may allow that the fact or evidence be proved by other facts. Such a statement is called a "Presumption". e.g. when there is sufficient proof that a person has been missing for at least seven (7) years after a diligent search for him, the law permits the presumption that he is dead.

The law further presumes that a person accused of an offence is innocent until his guilt is proven beyond reasonable doubts by a competent Body. This is an area that "talkative investigators" must be very cautious about. A little slip, and big trouble is born already. We do not judge anyone before proving him guilty or not guilty. Investigators are not Judges; their main duty is to **look for and bring up proofs or evidence** to help decide effectively on cases brought to their attention.

Other Presumptions are that

> (a) Judicial proceedings are properly conducted;
>
> (b) Public Officers have properly discharged their duties;
>
> (c) Letters, telegrams etc, properly dispatched were received by the addressees.

What is meant here is that all these are issues everybody, especially the Law Court, normally accepts as true without question.

Note that Presumptions are just substitutes for evidence and not the Evidence itself. They are roped in when direct evidence is lacking.

Presumptions may be *conclusive* or *rebuttable*. That is to say, presumptions may be convincing or may be initially accepted to be true but proved to be false later.

v.   ***Judicial Notice:*** There are many facts which do not have to be proved by Evidence because they are the subject of common knowledge. Everybody considers them to be true without any need to prove such facts. Examples include The Law itself, Natural Phenomena and Historical Facts. You will agree that no one needs to provide evidence as to whether the law is true or not. Everybody accepts the law as true. Ghana's Independence Day is "March 6, 1957". No one needs any proof of this fact before its acceptance. The Law takes *Judicial Notice* of these facts (i.e. Admits them without any further proofs).

Granted the Date Of Birth of a person is also March 6, 1957. This fact cannot be accepted anywhere on a silver platter; it will have to be proved beyond reasonable doubts, especially by the direct parents and/or genuine Statutory Documents, or otherwise. The Law Courts do not take any Judicial Notice of an individual's date of birth, generally.

A Natural Phenomenon that "the sun rises in the morning and sets in the evening" is also another common fact that does not need to be proved by anyone. It is simply true and cannot be challenged.

Investigations, or the Courts, readily accept such facts as true, BUT NOT SUBSTITUTES FOR EVIDENCE.

The purpose of *Judicial Notice* is to spare the Law Courts, as well as the parties concerned in a case, the expenses and time that would otherwise be consumed by trying to prove such indisputable facts.

PRIMA FACIE EVIDENCE

A *Prima Facie Evidence* is evidence based on what appears at first to be true without any further or deeper investigation. It is evidence that is just sufficient to establish something legally, unless it is found to be false later. Some people literally call it "surface evidence". Some investigators do not go beyond Prima Facie Evidence to conclude their investigations, as a practice. This is not the best.

PRIVILEGES

This is the *right to withhold evidence to protect an important interest or relationship*. For instance, an accused person cannot be forced to give Evidence against himself. We shall see later in this Book that in taking the Cautioned Statement of a suspect or accused, *neither of them is obliged to make a Statement unless he wishes to do so; besides, he is entitled to Counsel of his own choice.*

Another instance is the **right not to reveal** confidential communication between husband and wife, doctor and patient, father and son, etc.

So, under such circumstances, one has the right to withhold or refuse to give Evidence. This right is a privilege under the law and the investigator needs to bear all these in mind in his work. This Rule is however broken, perhaps strategically, by some investigators in the application of 2nd and 3rd Degrees of Interrogation (See the Chapter On Interrogation). That is not the best.

At least two things can happen later: Either the suspect/accused will say the "evidence" from him is not true but that he was placed under duress or torture OR the suspect/accused at a critical point will just make **"wrong confessions"** to investigators to deceive them.

This is one reason why the investigator must not compel a suspect or an accused person to provide evidence during interrogation. Even though there are various degrees of interrogation, they are just "principles" but not mandatory fast rules. Mind you, Principles are principles; common sense must always be applied to make them meaningful and more useful.

THE RELEVANCE OF EVIDENCE

This refers, generally, to the **usefulness** of specific pieces of evidence in specific investigation reports. Evidence, it should be noted, must relate to and help resolve an issue in dispute or under investigation. That is all.

Sometimes, however, it becomes absolutely relevant also to **exclude specific evidence** from investigation reports when it is very clear that such evidence can **prejudice or mislead decisions** on the case under investigation. For instance, Evidence that a particular suspect in a case *has previously committed murder*, may be excluded from a Report when it is likely to **prejudice** or **mislead decisions** on that case.

The *Relevance Of Evidence,* in common practice, is not a fast rule. The discretion of the investigator is more important. It should however be noted that this **does not** in any way suggest to any investigator to exclude vital evidence from Reports in exchange for bribe or any similar consideration.

SOURCES OF EVIDENCE

Every investigation has its own sources of evidence, depending on the task or issue under investigation.

Generally, however, sources of evidence include:

(a) Documents

(b) Photographs

(c) Offenders themselves (suspects/accused)

(d) Witnesses

(e) Informants, Collaborators, Sources, Agents

(f) Writings

(g) Public Records

(h) Bills

(i) Publications

(j) Personal Identification

(k) Crime Scene

HOW TO OBTAIN EVIDENCE

There are numerous ways by which Evidence can be obtained.

These include:

(i)   Interrogation

(ii)   Interviews

(iii)   Elicitation

(iv)   Confession

(v)   Search

(vi)   Research

(vii)   Inspection

(viii) Surveillance

(ix)   Examination

Interrogation: This is an act of obtaining required information or evidence by direct questioning and under conditions partly or fully controlled by the questioner or investigator (See the Chapter on Interrogation).

Interview: This is also an act of obtaining relevant information from a person by direct questioning but partly controlled by the interrogator.

Confession: This is a formal statement by a person to admit his guilt or involvement in an issue or to testify to the reality of a particular event under investigation.

Search: To 'search' means 'to go through and examine closely'. It may involve a person's physical body, house, office, farm, vehicle, bag, etc; and it may also involve the use of technical aids. This must always be guided by the law, however. (See the Chapter on Interrogation).

Research: This is "a careful study into something, somebody or an Institution in order to discover new facts or information". Here both covert and overt methods can be employed. It is normally used when it becomes necessary to, for instance, delve into the background of suspects, accused, witnesses, Organizations or documents/records critical to an investigation which are not readily available.

Examination: This refers to the critical study of documents as well as other objects or substances, marks, etc that have a bearing on the commission of an offence for evidence during investigation. Most of such examination are usually conducted by the use of technical aids and/or by experts. Furthermore, because *samples* of certain exhibits must be taken from the original for examination purposes, the original volumes or weights may not be fully preserved, but such reduction is usually just marginal or *relatively insignificant*.

Inspection: This mainly has to do with visits to crime scenes by investigators to have direct personal feel and observation of the intricacies of an incident in order to obtain relevant information on the crime or offence for subsequent interrogation, or other relevant action. It involves photographic or video recording of sites or crime scenes. Quite often, a lot of evidence abound at a crime scene, for instance, provided it is properly secured immediately after a crime is committed there. Work places, hotels or factories can also be inspected, by appropriate Statutory Agencies, for evidence on prohibited immigrants, tax evaders, terrorists, etc.

Surveillance: This is the secret watching of a person, group of persons, places, objects, Installations, *Organizations*, etc, in order to obtain useful information about them. It may be static, mobile, or the use of technical aids. It is mainly used in Secret Investigations and in Intelligence Practice. (See the notes on Secret Investigation).

PRESERVATION OF EVIDENCE

Investigators took custody of cocaine from a suspect and preliminary tests on the stuff (exhibit), on the day of the arrest, proved to be cocaine. Two days later when the investigators called for the same exhibit (properly labelled, of course), part of the whole thing had disappeared from the exhibits store while the rest had turned into a completely different substance. What happens?

There is clearly a very big problem, not only for the investigators, but for a lot more officers and the reputation of Service or Organization concerned.

It is therefore always very necessary for investigators to ensure that all exhibits are:

(i)   Accurately labelled. Here we are talking about the use of codified exhibit numbers in very high profile cases or the use of date, time, place where the stuff was seized; particulars of the apprehending Officer(s); nature of the substance seized; particulars of suspects; docket particulars, among others.

(ii)   Kept in a physically secured exhibit store.

(iii) Kept under Standard Temperatures and Pressures (STPs) as well as maintain their normal or original geometric conditions as at the time and place of seizure. For instance, you will not take a granulated substance into custody and the next day the whole thing dissolves into a different material.

CHAPTER 4

INTERROGATION

In all manner of investigations, at one stage or another, certain questions will be put and certain answers will be provided - even in medical investigations. This amounts to Interrogation. The main **"objective"** of this is **"to firmly establish the truth of allegations or uncertainties"**. It is to obtain concrete and reliable evidence from a human source to confirm a suspicion, or otherwise, through direct questioning.

In contemporary Criminal Investigations some Officers would just issue Police Statement Forms to suspects or witnesses right from the onset and ask them to give a Statement. That is not the best. It is better to first interrogate the suspect or witness, take down notes of important points and then urge the suspect or witness concerned to give his Statement in accordance with the answers he has provided at the interrogation, but, of course, voluntarily.

In this way the interrogator stands a better chance to obtain information relevant to the specific investigation on hand in which the suspect, witness or accused has or may have a case to answer. Otherwise, the suspect, accused or witness will just take the Statement Form and write any story at all for the investigator and of course, he will keep silent on information that may rather be vital to the specific investigation.

PREPARATION FOR INTERROGATION

The preparation for interrogation is subjective to specific tasks on hand. Generally, like any other human endeavour, there is a high tendency of deviating from the main "objective" of an exercise for lack of good preparation or planning. Since interrogation is itself a very critical factor in investigations, any deviation from the main "objective" can be very disastrous, eventually, in many ways. Painstaking efforts in preparation for interrogation is therefore paramount.

Lack of adequate preparation can result in the presentation of wrong Investigation Reports; but such Reports are, for instance, vital in the formulation of policies of Governments and other sensitive State Institutions. A whole State can even be misled quietly into taking very wrong decisions in diverse situations to embarrass itself.

When issues bothering on State Security especially are affected this way, the result can be a chaotic and an insecure society. The damaging effect of this trend of affairs on the economic development of a country can be any one's guess. Besides, there is also the likelihood of innocent and/or poor helpless people suffering various unfortunate fates including wrongful imprisonment.

Since Interrogation is a wholly strategic investigative activity whose success largely hinges on efficient and effective planning, a lot of critical factors need to be considered and these include:

(a) Classification

(b) Urgency of the task

(c) Terms Of Reference

(d) Venue for Interrogation

(e) Time for Interrogation

(f) Calibre, Number and Gender of Suspects, Accused, Witnesses

(g) Calibre, Number and Gender of Interrogators/Committee Of Enquiry Membership

(h) Security

(i) Independent Witnesses

(j) Medium of Communication

(k) Interpreters

(l) Dressing/Physical Appearance of Interrogators, Suspects, Accused, Witnesses.

(m) Transport and other Logistics

(n) The Questioning Process

(o) The Co-opting of Technocrats/other Professionals

(p) Background information of case, if possible

(q) Finance

(r) Escorts/Guards

(s) Available Information

(t) Method/Type of Interrogation

Classification

The reckless handling of a task by Officers has a tremendous impact on its success. Classification of tasks, either from its original source or by the 'recipient Body' determines the level of care that must be attached to every detailed aspect of a given task.

In the case of the latter, unclassified tasks may, among other things, be classified in respect of situations where:

(a) The Security of the State is at stake;

(b) The Personal Security of the President, Vice President, Speaker Of Parliament, Diplomat, or any other individual citizen of the country or foreigner legally resident or present in the country is at stake;

(c) Specific action needs to be taken by the State to prevent the commission of a serious crime or halt an insurgence;

(d) The Economy of the State can be at risk;

(e) At least, a Prima Facie evidence is urgently required to pave the way for a specific action to be taken in the interest of the State without offending the law.

Generally, as seen earlier in this book, classification may be: TOP SECRET, SECRET, RESTRICTED, CONFIDENTIAL OR PERSONAL, as the case may be.

Urgency Of Task

This must be considered first and foremost alongside "Classification". It has to do with the level of priority that has to be given to a task. That is, how much **time** and **resources** are available to complete a task in a record time or within the given time frame.

This always requires a very efficient and effective management of time and resources as well as the personal discipline of Officers handling the task in order to achieve the maximum possible best results.

The interrogator needs to adopt very efficient and effective techniques and/or strategies and ensure a very swift and effective re-adjustment of his personal and other equally important official programmes.

The more urgent a task is, the more extra care is needed in order to avoid "**critical errors**".

Meanwhile, the following may be useful for urgent interrogation tasks:

1. *Quick Confirmation Of Facts Provided:* This may sound irrelevant but ignoring it may be disastrous. Quickly contact your Superior Officer or whoever referred the case to you, if possible, for a quick confirmation of the content where and when certain aspects are not quite clear to the investigator. This is helpful for various reasons including:

   (a) It can give the investigator a better understanding of the task which in turn may help him plan and organize himself faster for the assignment.

   (b) There could be typographical errors in the preparation of the original signal to the investigator that might be misleading.

   (c) There could be errors in the syntax of the signal sent to the investigator. Such errors would definitely change the true meaning and facts of the signal so sent to the investigator to work on. A wrong Report could therefore be submitted in the end.

2. *Use Mainly Few Experienced Officers:* For urgent assignments especially, very few proven competent interrogators, about two or three in number, would be ideal. If too many interrogators are used, a lot more time might be required for the exercise.

3. *Pay Attention To Gender:* Where a female is involved in a case under investigation, ensure at least a competent lady is included on the team of interrogators or Committee Of Enquiry, as the case may be.

4. *Quick Plan Of Questions:* Even though an urgent interrogation exercise may be handled by competent Officers, the need to plan towards "questions" to ask is still necessary. There will for instance be the need to critically identify "FACTUAL AREAS" in the case under investigation and carefully and quickly determine the "order of questioning" or approach. Questions here are usually "very short and searching".

Assume, for instance, that three persons were arrested on suspicion of engaging in Armed Robbery and a quick interrogation of these suspects was required of you in order to obtain their Statements. The FACTUAL AREAS would include:

1. *What is the exact offence suspected or committed?*

2. *Whether any offensive weapons were found on any of them after searching; and if yes,*

3. *What are the makes, models and sources of supply of these weapons? Are they licensed by the Police?*

4. *Where was each of the suspects picked up, under what circumstance and by whom?*

5. *What is the extent of involvement of each of them in the case, among others.*

These would help determine where and how to start the questioning from, for each of them; and even among the suspects, accused or witnesses, who among them should be questioned first and in what order; what question(s) should be directed to who, and at what stage of the interrogation, etc, so as to bring out the best possible results.

If, however, a clearly good job is done and yet Superior Officers require further interrogation, after presenting a final Report, so be it.

5. *Intent And Action:* There is always a reason for one to act in a certain manner, be it

Criminal or otherwise. These are the critical areas of interrogation and where also

Criminal Laws are usually applied for conviction. Thus, interrogators need to very precisely establish these for each individual under investigation and bring them out very clearly in a report to enable informed decisions to be taken on them.

Governments, organisations and individuals lose a number of very good cases in the Law Courts partly due to the failure or "unwillingness" of investigators (including Committees Of Enquiry) to VERY CLEARLY ESTABLISH such import during interrogation or investigation.

6. *Submission Of Interim Report:* For very urgent assignments, it may be required to quickly submit Interim Reports. That must throw sufficient light on the initial facts or evidence established. *{See the chapter on "Evidence"}.*

TERMS OF REFERENCE

This refers to what exactly an exercise seeks to establish or is required to prove or disprove. One cannot miss the mark here, and should not. Every form of planning of an interrogation depends on the Terms Of Reference (TOR).

Let us consider an example:

"Five persons are feared dead, while six others sustained gunshot wounds, during clashes between COTT and the MILL tribes at FIXX, a village near SOCC in the Northern Region of an Island. The disturbances that occurred on Sunday night were caused by a misunderstanding between some COTT and MILL over a piece of land meant for the construction of a hospital. Both ethnic groups claim ownership of the land and want compensation paid to them. The issue degenerated into violence, which was characterized by sporadic shooting and the burning down of about a hundred houses. No arrests have been made so far."

Supposing you were asked to interrogate three persons only suspected of involvement (but not formally arrested) in the above newspaper reported case and establish:

(a) *The exact cause of the clashes;*

(b) *The exact identities of persons who initiated the clashes;*

(c) *The types of weapon used in the clashes;*

(d) *The exact number and breakdown of casualties and extent of damage to other property and*

(e) *Make appropriate recommendations to forestall any such future occurrence.*

These requirements are the TERMS OF REFERENCE for this specific assignment. The TOR spells out what exactly is required of an interrogation or investigation. It is always very essential for the interrogator to KNOW and UNDERSTAND VERY CLEARLY the TOR before proceeding to tackle the job on hand.

In an advanced situation, however, the TOR would have to be determined by the interrogator. For instance, supposing in the above newspaper reported case, instruction from the Superior Officer to the investigator read: *"Investigate this story and report immediately."*

In such a situation, the investigator has to determine the "factual areas" himself. That is, areas or aspects of the case deemed necessary to explore so as to bring up a sensible and useful Report.

VENUE FOR THE INTERROGATION

For purposes of security and distraction, the investigator needs to select reasonably good venues for interrogation irrespective of its urgency.

Factors that need to be carefully considered here include:

(a) The prevailing or anticipated conditions in the specific as well as general environment of the venue for interrogation;

(b) The set up of the interrogation room itself.

The set up should be conducive, at the discretion of the interrogator, for a smooth peaceful and successful exercise, granted that the second and third degrees of interrogation would not necessarily be brought to play.

The normal interrogation room should sufficiently be devoid of distraction and anything scaring. Except for Operational Purposes, electronic gadgets and equipment should be tuned very low or off completely.

The use of **CONGESTED OFFICES** should be avoided also for professional and security reasons. Persons who do not have anything to do with the interrogation should not be present during interrogation, it does not matter whether they are colleague Officers or not. (*See Distraction in Chapter 9*).

THE NUMBER, GENDER AND CALIBRE OF SUSPECTS/WITNESSES

The "Number" refers to the list of persons to be interrogated. This can increase in the course of interrogation and calls for the order of interrogation discussed earlier. "Gender" refers to whether suspects/witnesses are ALL-FEMALE, ALL-MALE or a composition of both sexes. This in turn influences the balance in the composition of the team of interrogators or Committee Of Enquiry. In the case of "Calibre", as seen earlier also, a little knowledge about the personality of the suspect or witness helps to determine the type of questions to ask the individual, how to ask such questions and when.

SECURITY ARRANGEMENT

One does not take chances in the conduct of interrogation. There is always the need to:

(a) Secure the exercise itself. Care should be taken to ensure the SECRECY of the exercise. Avoid the use of Congested Offices for interrogation and insist on the Need To Know Rule.

(b) Secure the suspects, accused and witnesses. Any of them can be attacked by aggrieved persons surprisingly, depending on the nature of the task, for instance. The fact that any of those in custody can escape during interrogation cannot also be ruled out. Any of them can feign insanity and attack the interrogators out of the blue.

(c) Secure the investigator since he can also be attacked by aggrieved parties or even the suspect being interrogated, depending on the nature of the job on hand.

(d) Secure the venue. Can the venue for interrogation be available for full use throughout the entire exercise (not partial use as we know of Congested Offices). Can the place offer the necessary safeguards for Officers during interrogation or in case of any emergency? Such situations must be carefully considered, as much as possible.

INDEPENDENT WITNESSES

Independent Witnesses are a very important component of a typical interrogation exercise. They are more or less observers who provide a legal "balance or check", if you like, between interrogators on one side and suspects/witnesses/accused on the other. They are not involved in the case under investigation but just observers. They are not part of the team of interrogators either.

Independent Witnesses are however legally required during interrogation in criminal cases. Theirs is to observe and endorse proceedings during interrogation and might be called in to clear the air, should there arise any doubts as regards the mode of an interrogation. They should not be relations of suspects, accused or witnesses and they are not to ask any questions, provide answers or pass any comments whatsoever at the interrogation.

The choice of Independent Witnesses depends on the nature of the job on hand. It also depends on the medium of communication to be used in the exercise, the gender of suspects and witnesses as well as the moral values of the individual Independent Witness in terms of secrecy, punctuality, motivation, among others.

Medium of Communication

This refers to the language to be used in an interrogation. Interrogators, suspects, witnesses, accused persons and Independent Witnesses, at every single session, must all be very conversant with the medium of communication.

It may involve the use of the Sign Language (for the deaf and dumb) or any normal spoken language.

In a very helpless situation, there is the need to engage the services of a reliable interpreter to serve as a communication facilitator or bridge. Such arrangement needs to be made very swiftly, but cautiously, in order not to stall the interrogation on hand.

Note that sometimes a suspect or witness can obviously speak, say, fluent English, yet can insist on the use of a different language, say, Efutu or Dagbani. Here, the interrogator has to oblige and quickly make the necessary arrangement for an Interpreter and an Independent Witness conversant with such language, if necessary.

A complex situation arises when "multi-languages" are involved. That is where suspects and witnesses can only express themselves in many individual different languages. That is, supposing one has to interrogate, say, three witnesses and two suspects in a criminal case who are all of different nationalities.

Granted that each of these suspects and witnesses claims to speak and understand only their respective national languages, for instance, English,

Spanish or Arabic, the interrogator, in the circumstance, will have to arrange within the shortest possible time, for either:

(a) A reliable Interpreter who is very conversant with all three languages to be used for all the suspects and witnesses OR

(b) A reliable Interpreter for each, or any two, of the languages of the suspects and witnesses.

The issue of an Independent Witness will also have to be considered in the same perspective.

Having a multi-lingual interrogator on the panel fluent in all these languages will be a special advantage here.

Note, however, that the interrogator cannot solely decide and impose the medium of communication for an interrogation on suspects or witnesses. That is never done. The choice of language or medium of communication by a suspect or witness has to be respected by the investigator at all times as their preserved right in the case under investigation.

PHYSICAL APPEARANCE (DRESSING)

The physical appearance of interrogators, suspects, accused persons, witnesses and co-opted participants in an interrogation can distract. Decency is encouraged at all times. (See the chapter on Distraction).

TECHNICAL AIDS

These have to be used with much circumspection or very professionally. Nevertheless, over-reliance on technical aids can sometimes spring unfortunate surprises for the investigator. These are machines that can develop technical faults or even break down at any time without warning. There is therefore the need to always devise appropriate back-up mechanisms to take care of such eventualities and not to lose vital information provided at such a bugged interrogation.

RELIABLE TRANSPORT

This becomes necessary in interrogation mainly in anticipation of:

(a) When suspects in custody suddenly fall ill and must be rushed to a good health facility for the necessary medical attention; and

(b) When suspects in custody have to be transported from a distance to and from the interrogation centre.

TYPES AND ORDER OF QUESTIONING

See the notes under *Calibre, Number and Gender of Suspects and Witnesses.*

NEED TO CO-OPT TECHNOCRATS

See the notes on *The Questioning Process.*

BACKGROUND INFORMATION ON THE CASE

This helps mainly when it comes to making recommendation on the case investigated. Any background information so obtained on a case under investigation should only be applied WITHOUT ANY PREJUDICE WHATSOEVER. Such information may also be helpful in the planning of the entire investigation or at least the interrogation.

STAND-BY ESCORTS/GUARDS

This is necessary in case a suspect, suddenly, has to be taken into custody or when there is the need to provide guard services to suspects already in custody to the interrogation centre and back to cells.

They are also important in case a suspect, witness, or accused has to be taken to hospital for medical attention or when there is the need for any of these to attend to nature's call. Both female and male escorts are required, subject to the gender of the suspects, accused persons and witnesses involved.

METHOD/TYPE OF INTERROGATION TO USE

Depending on the nature or specific circumstance of an interrogation, one needs to decide on the type or method of interrogation to be adopted for an assignment. This may be FIRST, SECOND, OR THIRD DEGREE INTERROGATION, as the case may be. Much care must always be taken to keep within the law. The preferred choice is the First Degree Interrogation. *{See Degrees Of Interrogation}.*

AVAILABILITY OF FUNDS AND LOGISTICS

Funds and Logistics are always needed to take care of contingencies during investigation, if and only if efficiency is anything to go by. At least the Interrogators, Co-opted Technocrats, Interpreters, Independent Witnesses and 'Vital' Witnesses in a case will have to be well-motivated to make themselves available to the exercise on hand and to give off their best at the same time. They may be needed in subsequent cases.

THE 'OBJECTIVE' OF INTERROGATION

Much care must be taken not to confuse *The Objective* of an interrogation with its *Terms Of Reference (TOR)*, even though they appear the same.

The latter points to a set of facts or information that the investigator must bring up, establish or disprove. These facts are raw materials to be used in decision making or policy formulation, at higher levels, to achieve a *certain* OBJECTIVE in the interest of society or the State.

We see here then that the TOR feeds into or fuels the OBJECTIVE of an investigation but it may not sound so simple to understand the difference between the two.

When suspects in criminal cases are interrogated, for instance, the main OBJECTIVE is not necessarily to impose Court Fines on them, imprison them, or get their identities in Court Records as being criminals. That is not the case. Merely committing people to prison is not the real answer, even though this book recognizes the relative impact of reform in prisons. **The real social problems pushing people to prison need to be tackled effectively and that must be the OBJECTIVE of every interrogation or investigation.**

The real issue at stake is to *determine the modus operandi of suspects for specific crimes in order to LIMIT or DO AWAY with such behaviour from the society, thereby injecting sanity into the populace and eventually building mutual confidence in one another for peaceful co-existence and governance.*

If criminals or other offenders of the law are not properly interrogated to efficiently and effectively determine their Methods of Operation and appropriate measures adopted to limit or do away with such behaviour in society or in governance, if you like, peaceful society and governance will remain a mirage.

The real objective of interrogation is therefore to solve problems that THREATEN OR CAN THREATEN THE PEACE OF SOCIETY OR THE SECURITY OF A STATE.

That is why interrogation, at all levels, including Committees of Enquiry, must be handled by experts in the profession and not just anybody.

For these reasons, this Book places special emphasis on the qualities of an interrogator; not everyone can interrogate appropriately on issues that have a bearing on State Security for instance, irrespective of a person's official position, popularity or political party affiliation. Proven competence matters here. (*See the Chapter on Modus Operandi*).

ACCESS TO INFORMATION

It is very necessary for an Interrogator to look for vital information from a wide range of sources of information, apart from the crime scene, to enhance the quality of questions to ask each suspect/witness in a specific interrogation. Good access to such sources of information must be strategized. So, in every situation or for every task, an interrogator needs to ask himself, for instance:

1. What is my level of ACCESS to the information I need?

2. How RELIABLE is the source of such information?

3. How RELIABLE is the person providing such information from its source?

4. Do such persons have good and DIRECT ACCESS to the information I require?

5. Can they really provide the needed evidence within the required time?

6. Will they be available at the required time?

NOTE that these refer to checks made on the quiet by the interrogator in respect of every task given him, where and when possible.

Someone may clearly have very useful information or evidence relating to an important issue under investigation but may not be prepared to provide such information. How do we get such a person to provide the evidence so badly needed for the success of our work?

On the other hand, another source may be willing to provide the needed information, but may not be available at the right time that such information is needed, and so on.

These issues all need to be factored into the planning of the exercise on hand and given the needed attention to enhance its success.

THE VALUE OF INFORMATION

The value of every piece of information is determined by three main factors, namely:

1. *Reliability:* The interrogator must ensure that every piece of information he is working with is TRUE and if so, to what extent can one depend on it.

2. *Accuracy:* If even the information is true, how PRECISE or exact is it for efficient and effective use? Suspects, accused and witnesses sometimes tell half-truths (or polished ones), and the investigator must watch out for that, lest he is swindled.

3. *Timeliness:* Information can be Reliable and Accurate by all standards, but if it is not provided or used at the appropriate time, it loses its value and hence becomes worthless altogether.

PERSONAL INTERESTS

This is an occupational hazard, especially for investigators. The real danger is where an interrogator directly in charge of a case has such personal interest in a case on hand. Where and when this happens to be the case, the entire interrogation or investigation is already jeopardized, if not compromised.

Such attitude can sometimes also be influenced by pressures from Political Authorities, Old Students Unions, Clubs, Family Relations and Immoral Considerations, among others.

Where a person is vulnerable, in this respect, it is better he stays out of the entire exercise for the purpose of safeguarding his integrity in the spirit of professionalism. It should be of grave concern for an interrogator not to allow himself to be constrained by any means to limit THE NUMBER AND TYPE OF QUESTIONS TO ASK A SUSPECT OR ACCUSED. If an interrogator cannot overcome the weight of external pressures from influential persons, as indicated above, it is always better he does not take part at all in that particular job, it must be emphasized.

A weak investigator will not ask very obvious simple questions that can bring out important facts or truths in relation to the case under investigation. This is very very bad and unprofessional and, of course, not helpful eventually.

Sometimes too, an investigator in a case has a bone to pick with a suspect in the case he is handling. The tendency of the investigator saying within himself: "…Ahaa…I've got him this time and I'll teach him a lesson…" and truly going ahead to 'work out' the conviction of the 'helpless', is not the best.

WHO INTERROGATES? : THE INTERROGATOR

Not everyone can interrogate, as seen earlier, when it comes to matters bothering on State Security, Public figures and/or 'helpless' individuals. A professionally competent interrogator must have certain personal and professional qualities and capabilities that places him in the right perspective for such tasks.

There are times when simple interrogation exercises degenerate, unfortunately, into SUMMARY TRIALS, QUARRELS or VIOLENCE. Good qualities of an interrogator will certainly avoid all that and safeguard the objective of the investigation.

Interrogation should therefore be conducted in such a manner that at the end of the day the main OBJECTIVE is achieved without, necessarily, creating any or too many enemies for one's self.

Below are some of the qualities of a good interrogator.

1. ***Self-Confidence:*** A good interrogator must always be confident on the job. He must be bold and exert efficient and effective control over the exercise. He must know exactly what he is looking for and how exactly to work towards that and achieve the maximum best possible results.

    Lack of confidence usually sets in when the interrogator is perhaps fresh on the job, habitually incompetent or "doing his own thing". Other times, lack of confidence sets in when the interrogator loses focus or when he becomes subservient to or intimidated by certain interested political authority or by the social status of the person under interrogation, or the credentials of suspects' relations, among others.

Honesty, truth, fairness and objectivity on the job builds confidence.

2. ***Retentive Memory:*** If the interrogator easily forgets, he is not likely to gather sufficient facts since he cannot write every answer that is provided by suspects or witnesses during an interrogation. He will not be able also to compare answers well at different sittings or times and direct appropriate responses to the suspect or witness concerned, when necessary. He cannot turn on the appropriate flexibilities, or heat, to achieve maximum possible best results. Having a good retentive memory will save the interrogator from such problems. It helps the interrogator when a suspect provides different answers for the same question at different times and in many other ways.

    Let me just repeat here that, yes, electronic devices can be used to record interrogation, operationally, when circumstances so demand. But, that is not always hundred percent helpful. (See "Planning" in Chapter 2).

3. ***Humane:*** Being friendly to people, no matter the circumstances, pays a lot. When a suspect appears before an interrogator for interrogation, that does not mean the interrogator should treat the suspect with contempt or as an enemy. No!! Being friendly and making the suspect feel recognized as a human being has a lot of psychological influence that can, to a reasonably good extent, play to the advantage of the investigator, in as much as the task on hand is concerned. Even though that may not necessarily apply to every operative circumstance, it certainly pays.

4. ***Moral Uprightness:*** (See the Chapter on Planning).

5. ***Bridling The Tongue:*** Information disclosed during interrogation, or investigation, must be treated as classified. An interrogator who goes out to spread what he has heard in an interrogation, or investigation, places his own life, job and reputation at a huge risk, not even to mention his Organization or State.

6. ***Language:*** The ability to understand and speak many languages is an advantage for every interrogator. If for nothing at all, the problem of having to hurriedly look for reliable interpreters when the need arises, can be limited or even ruled out on many occasions. It should be noted that a co-opted interpreter cannot exactly interpret the real views or opinions of the investigator at an interrogation, no matter how good that interpreter might be.

7. ***Knowledge:*** At least a fairly good knowledge in a wide range of areas of social, economic, or other fields of human endeavour places an interrogator at an advantage when dealing with issues that require such experience. The interrogator will for instance not be found wanting in the use of terminology and/or technicalities that might otherwise confuse an ordinary person.

8. ***Personal Skills And Experience:*** 'Flexibility' is a pleasant combination of Principles, Skills and Experience on the job. It is a very important ingredient in the conduct of investigations, or interrogation. The more flexible an investigator is, the more

successful he can be on the job, generally. Flexibility is however subject to the level of personal experience of the investigator on the job. The more experienced and skilful an investigator is on the job, the more flexible, efficient and effective the exercise can go. {See "Selecting Officers For Interrogation/Committees Of Enquiry" below}.

9. ***Promises And Gifts:*** It is not good for an interrogator to make any promise whatsoever to a suspect, accused, witness or their relations in any case under investigation at any time and under any circumstance. Besides being woefully unethical, the investigator who does that might be "signing his own death warrant!!" Similarly, the investigator must watch out for offers both in kind and in cash from suspects/witnesses or their relations and stay very clear off them and save himself from possible embarrassment in future.

10. ***Dressing:*** The dressing or general appearance of the interrogator has an impact on the interrogation he might be handling on a particular occasion. (See the Chapter on Planning).

11. ***Bias And Emotions:*** It is unprofessional to introduce personal emotions into cases under investigation or interrogation. That is a first step towards bias. Some investigators have the tendency of listening to only one side of the case, usually the "favourite" side, and then straightaway write the final Report. That is also very bad. The investigator needs to **take pains to carefully LISTEN EXHAUSTIVELY to every person connected to the case under investigation** before setting out to write his Report.

12. ***Choice Of Words:*** The choice of words, especially on the part of the investigator, is a very delicate issue in interrogation. The wrong framing of questions as well as the use of "unmerited" words on suspects or witnesses can inflame passions at an interrogation. It can lead to a clash between the interrogator and suspect or witness. This, certainly, will defeat the objective of the investigation.

At the same time, the investigator needs to be alert to the choice of words by suspects, accused or witnesses and should handle same with much circumspection. This is an area where the personal skills and experience of the investigator become essential. Suspects, accused or witnesses can, strategically, make "wrong choice of words" sometimes to deliberately provoke the anger of the investigator and ultimately frustrate the conduct of the interrogation.

These are critical issues that must concern every investigator.

SELECTING OFFICERS FOR INTERROGATION/ MEMBERSHIP OF COMMITTEES OF ENQUIRY

The discussion here is just in furtherance of that of the *"Qualities Of A Good Interrogator"* seen above. Those qualities are all required in the choice of Officers for interrogation or in the selection of Members of a Committee of Enquiry or Jury. Any **carelessness** here can ruin their real purposes and victimize innocent and/or helpless poor people, to say the least.

One dares stress here that in certain situations, Officers are just chosen to handle very important interrogation exercises or to sit on Committees Of Enquiry by virtue of their political affiliation to the ruling government, their high ranks, or "who can sing the master's song well". Such choices, without prejudice, may not be the best. What matters most is COMPETENCE. None of these status, on their own, spells competence just like that. Where competence is lacking, truth can easily be compromised for such "expediencies". And, whenever "truth" is compromised, in any shade, the real objective of the exercise is also inevitably compromised. Systems that really mean business do not go this way for the development of their constituencies.

"ANYTHING GOES, IT IS JUST A MATTER OF PRESENTING SOMETHING" or yet still, "let's do something to represent something…", and views like that can only be found in weak, compromised and inept minds.

When selecting Officers for interrogation, to sit on a Committee Of Enquiry or on a Jury, it is also necessary for the selecting authority to **understand the CONTENT and know the IMPORT of the issues to be investigated, if such Authority is not the ORIGINATOR of the task.** This has a direct bearing on the type of persons to select for a given task at a given time. *{See Planning in Chapter 2}.*

We may briefly add the following in making the appropriate choices:

(a) ***Good Knowledge Of Subject Area:*** This is one of the very first things a Superior Officer, or Selecting Officer, considers in choosing Officers to interrogate suspects or to sit on a Committee Of Enquiry or Jury. In the conduct of an investigation that involves BALLISTICS for instance, the choice of investigators or persons to sit on a Committee of Enquiry should be people who are known to have PROVEN EXPERIENCE IN BALLISTICS, and not necessarily high ranks, political affiliation with the government in power or any similar consideration as mentioned above. Such disregard to basic principles is one of the unnoticed root causes of numerous conflicts and other chaotic situations we find around. But, where none of the interrogators in the Organization is conversant with the subject area of a specific investigation, then a reliable technocrat **in the appropriate subject area** will have to be co-opted to assist. Of course, he must be well motivated, as seen in an earlier discussion.

(b) ***Experience:*** By 'experience' in interrogation we mean *the extent of one's diligent practical involvement in interrogation over a reasonable period of apprenticeship under responsible supervision and direction.* The more one practically gets involved and accepts correction on the job, the more he builds up experience. Take note that it is not just the number of years that a person has worked with an Organization that deals with interrogation that makes one an experienced person on the job - NEVER! That is deceptive. It is rather the person's **diligent involvement, under responsible supervision over a reasonable period of time,** as indicated above, that matters. So we see that **when we truly mean business**, ranks alone cannot be the determining factor to put someone on a sensitive interrogation exercise or Committee Of Enquiry. If otherwise, then so be it. There are various other advantages in the preference of experienced Officers for Interrogation, Committee Of Enquiry or Jury. These may be realized in areas such as:

TIME: An experienced Officer is more likely to complete an urgent task in time or within schedule.

MISTAKES/ERRORS: Experienced Officers are more likely to make less mistakes, especially when working under pressure or when required to complete an assignment in a very limited time.

SUPERVISION/DIRECTION: Experienced Officers will not need much supervision or direction.

EFFICIENCY AND EFFECTIVENESS: These have to do with the good management of the twists and turns peculiar to an exercise in order to produce the best possible results. The more experienced an Officer is the more capable he is to handle such complex situations. It is always good to have enough experienced Officers on a Panel of Interrogators, Committee of Enquiry or Jury, as the case may be. It is, nevertheless, very ideal to mingle one or two inexperienced but very promising Officers with the experienced ones so that they can understudy the latter on the job.

(c) ***Power Of Observation and Discernment:*** Interrogation does not just involve questioning. It also goes with a very careful observation of the individual being questioned at any particular point in time, since gestures speak volumes about an individual. This requires much experience in observation and discernment to handle.

There must always be a specific strategic order of questioning for each individual suspect, accused or witness, and for each case and at any particular point in time, as seen earlier under "Planning".

Now, as you are questioning a suspect or an offender to bring out certain facts from the person, that person is also constantly calculating and strategizing ways and means to outwit you the investigator, if he knows within himself that he is actually guilty or involved in the offence.

It takes an experienced investigator quite conversant with *Interrogation Techniques* to sail through such situations neatly and bring up good results. {*Interrogation Techniques* is discussed in **"PRINCIPLES OF INTERROGATION"** also written by this Author and published by AuthorHouse Publishers, Bloomington, USA}.

Now, what do we say about 'Observation'? This even requires more experience to do than questioning. An experienced interrogator should be able to tell when a person under interrogation is lying and when he is telling the truth (*but of course without letting the suspect know*}. This will help him know how to direct further questions to the suspect or witness, among other things.

(d) **Background Knowledge:** This helps to determine the **type** and **order** of questions to ask, and **how to present** such questions. Not just that but it also helps the interrogator to anticipate a suspect's or witness' response or reaction to specific questions and to know how to deal effectively with such response.

Sometimes the specific case under investigation had come to notice before and one or two of the persons involved had been investigated for a similar or other offence some time past. In such situations, unless the Officers who handled the previous interrogation or investigation were clearly found to have misconducted themselves in that exercise, they might be good materials to handle the current interrogation.

(e) ***Rank:*** We discussed 'Rank' earlier. We however emphasize that, when it comes to critical *work output*, it is <u>individual competence</u> that matters most and that should not be compromised, under any circumstance, if excellent results are truly required.

(f) ***Availability:*** When charging someone with the responsibility of interrogation, or investigation, the availability of the person throughout the exercise needs to be carefully taken into consideration. It is not worthwhile to consider an Officer who will not have time for the job and hence not get the Report ready within the required time frame. An Officer who has got too much work on hand or is a habitual "busy-body", needs to be rested when it comes to very important tasks.

(g) ***Temperament:*** The temperament of an Officer is also very important when it comes to selecting people for interrogation. The higher the temperament of an Officer the more likely he is to turn the interrogation into a confrontation or even a "trial".

But note, that an interrogation is not a trial. The interrogation room itself is not a Court Room. Interrogating someone does not mean such a person is guilty of the offence under investigation. It is the Law Courts that decide on guilt after a fair trial.

(h) ***General Mood:*** The general mood in which an Officer finds himself at any point in time has a lot of influence or, if you like, impact on his work at that material time. This should equally be considered carefully in selecting persons to conduct interrogation or sit on a Committee Of Enquiry or Jury. Here we are looking at issues like bereavement, divorce, robbery, a Serious Court Case, Ejection from Residence and similar problems that can effectively have a telling effect on the investigator, sometimes over a period of time, as human as he is. By human nature, an Officer facing such problems is likely to translate any of these into his work. Hence if an Officer is genuinely challenged with such or other problems and decides to opt out of an investigation, he might be allowed. On the other hand, if an Officer cannot so easily be excused on a Panel then sitting might have to be adjourned to an appropriate date that will see every member present for normal business to proceed. For instance, in a recent Case brought before The Supreme Court of a certain country by a Political Party against the Government in respect of a Constitutional Provision for the implementation of Free Compulsory Universal Basic Education (FCUBE), judgement in the Case had to be deferred to a more convenient time by The Supreme Court citing the <u>bereavement</u> of a Member of the seven-man Panel Of Judges that sat on the case.

(i) **Health:** The health of an Officer is also very important in selecting persons for interrogation. Someone who suffers from, say, epilepsy, cannot be a good material for interrogation because he can collapse at any time and spoil the exercise. A known sickler may obviously not be a good material for interrogation. Besides, investigators need to regularly check their health status, eat well, have enough rest every week and exercise regularly to stay healthy at all times. Occasional pleasure trips may not be too bad to refresh the mind.

(j) **Reliability:** A good Officer for interrogation should be one proven to bring up Reliable, Accurate and Timely Reports after every task. Indeed, such an Officer can be counted on. A professionally reliable Officer will not for instance go about divulging information to undesirables. He certainly will not be a drunkard or one who sleeps on duty; such people have relatively weak minds. One cannot just ignore these issues in selecting Officers for Interrogation or Investigation, generally.

SELECTION OF INDEPENDENT WITNESSES

For the purposes of protecting information and enhancing successful interrogation, the selection of Independent Witnesses in interrogation must be very carefully done. The necessary precautions must be taken to ensure that information provided at the interrogation, or whatever goes on there, *remains in the interrogation room strictly.* His specific role at an interrogation must be clearly spelt out to him for strict compliance. He does not take part in the interrogation. He is just to observe, and only that.

It is important to let an Independent Witness know the GRAVITY and/or CONSEQUENCES of any leakage of information provided at or relating to any investigation they witness. Sometimes it pays to secretly monitor such Independent Witnesses for some reasonable time *before* and *after* taking part in an interrogation, or *during* such an exercise, if it has to be conducted in series over a period of time. If such precautions are not taken, mind you, any leakage of information that eventually goes to adversely affect the interrogation can be placed squarely at the doorstep of the interrogator. This needs to be avoided.

<u>THE CHOICE OF INTERPRETERS</u>

The choice of Interpreters also needs to be very carefully made. Such co-opted persons virtually take active part in the actual interrogation or have access to vital information. They are not on the same pedestal as Independent Witnesses who will just sit in the interrogation and <u>observe</u> proceedings. Interpreters actually take part in the interrogation itself and therefore need to be very carefully selected. They only do not originate any questions at the sitting and cannot also control the exercise, unlike the actual interrogators. {See "Planning"}.

Unless, and again unless, any of the Officers on the interrogation team has a 'hidden knowledge' of or secretly understands the medium of communication for which the services of an interpreter has been sought, sympathies in certain situations, and human nature as it is, can compel an interpreter to even ask suspect not to disclose certain vital information in that language that is 'supposedly' not understood by any of the interrogators, and for which an interpreter has been invited. This is not speculation, but something that happens in actual practice. So, extra care must be taken in engaging any Interpreter for investigation purposes.

SECRECY IN INTERROGATION

It is extremely important for an Interrogator to be able to keep secrets in as much as cases brought to his attention are concerned. That is to say, the interrogator should not unnecessarily disclose any information that has to do with cases or issues that he:

(a) Has conducted interrogation on;

(b) Is about to conduct interrogation on; or

(c) Is conducting interrogation on.

Only those who NEED TO KNOW should know. This is the Principle of Compartmentation (in intelligence practice) otherwise known as NTK. It must be rigidly embraced by every interrogator or Member of a Committee Of Enquiry, as professional practice demands; all in the interest of the interrogators themselves, first and foremost. Any violation of this Principle has a high potential of jeopardizing the entire investigation (not just the interrogation), apart from the likelihood of producing a bogus Report in the end. Other dire consequences in violating NTK are:

(a) *Loss of vital Evidence*

(b) *" " very important Witnesses*

(c) *Misleading Information could be provided by suspects, accused, etc.*

(d) *Violence or Conflicts between opposing factions could be provoked.*

(e) *There could be public scare to provide/volunteer useful information to the Investigator's Organization.*

(f) *Embarrassment could be caused for Governments, Organizations and Individuals, sometimes irreparably.*

(g) *The actual purpose of the exercise will be compromised.*

THE QUESTIONING PROCESS

Before you begin questioning, it is important to **cross-check whether the accused, suspect or witness is aware of why he is to be questioned**. The Law generally requires that a person under investigation must know why he is under investigation.

Now, questioning is an art. It must begin somewhere and end smoothly at another point usually in a distinct pattern. In other words it must be orderly and very clear in presentation. The investigators need to KNOW and UNDERSTAND VERY WELL WHAT THE EXACT REQUIREMENT OF THE INVESTIGATION IS. This will assist them to know *what type of questions to ask, when to ask what, how to ask what* and *why ask what question,* and so on.

Searching questions are mostly asked. These are usually short, straightforward and compelling. For *example*:

What happened?, How?, Who said it?, Can you explain?, Why?, When? Who? Etc.

In certain instances, direct statements can be made by the interrogator for the one being interrogated to respond or comment. It is an effective form of provoking or compelling people, if you like, to provide information. Even though they normally require question tags, these tags are usually left out in interrogation. For instance:

1. *You were not at the Bank, were you?* (Common English). In interrogation you can just say: *"You were not at the Bank "*, and leave it there for the suspect or witness to respond.

2. *The money was found on you, wasn't it?* (Common English). For our purpose, we say: *"The money was found on you"*, and leave it there for the suspect to respond.

3. *You saw the Chief Justice, didn't you?* (Common English). For our purpose, we say: *"You saw the Chief Justice"*, and leave it there for the suspect to react.

Note that there is nothing wrong using question tags in interrogation. They are however deliberately left out strategically due to the psychological impact that that can have on the suspect or witness. Lawyers, Prosecutors and Judges employ the strategy a lot during cross-examination; and they get very good results. Long questions may not be too helpful. Such can even end up confusing the suspects or witnesses, and in some instances, the interrogator himself asking the question can also get mixed-up. *(See the Chapter on Planning).*

Mind you, questioning should be done in a reasonably low tone; not as commands or orders. Most people do not like to be ordered or commanded, so when they are treated in such a manner, passions can be inflamed. That in turn may not be good for an interrogation.

INTERROGATING MORE THAN ONE PERSON

Generally, where and when all the parties to be interrogated are in custody, the ideal thing the interrogator must do is to ensure that those suspects are kept *completely separate* from each other or one another without regard to whether there is space or not to accommodate them at the Station handling the investigation. The necessary arrangement must be made for this in nearby Detention Facilities, but a close eye must be kept on them still by the Officers handling the Case. It is always important for investigators to ensure that there is adequate detention facilities before taking suspects to custody. There are exceptional cases, however. *{See "Arrests, Search And Detention}*

Then, in the actual interrogation, **only one person** (accused, suspect or witness) should be interrogated at a time; the rest should be kept reasonably far away from the interrogation room so as not to make them privy to anything whatsoever that might take place at the interrogation until their respective turns. Then also, after a person is interrogated, he is not taken back to join his other accomplices, but still kept separately from those yet to be interrogated, *except for special operational reasons.* They could confer and hide a lot of very important information or evidence.

After interrogating one person at a time, sometimes *conflicting answers* are provided by the same or different persons. When conflicting answers are provided by the same person, the person would have to be interrogated again on those conflicting answers. The same question(s) for which conflicting answers have been provided by the suspect would be asked again but this time more *carefully reframed* for the purpose of clarification.

CONFRONTATION

When two or more persons involved in a case provide conflicting answers to an issue, the situation is different. Here, the interrogator would *very carefully arrange to meet the affected suspects or persons together at the same time and place using a very good Cover Story.*

In other words, each person would be invited separately without letting the other party know about it. An Independent Witness MUST BE PRESENT. He shall also be invited "secretly". *The actual or true objective of all these invitations will NOT BE DISCLOSED TO ANY OF THESE PEOPLE INVITED.* Only those who need to know should know.

Adequate arrangement would have to be made by the investigator to receive each of these persons separately, except those in custody who can be brought in at the instance of the investigator.

This 'System' is called a CONFRONTATION in Interrogation.

The following need to be considered very carefully in trying to organize a Confrontation:

(a) Invitation

(b) Timing

(c) Purpose

(d) Venue

(e) Security

(f) Independent Witness.

(g) Interpreters

(a) ***Invitation:*** In setting out to invite persons for a "Confrontation", one needs to *assess and strategize* on how to quietly invite each person involved, granted that such persons so required for the Confrontation are not in custody; they could be suspects on bail, or witnesses in private locations. Persons in custody are always available (if only they have not broken jail) and are more easily accessible.

We need to ask ourselves:

(i)   *Where can the person be located?*

(ii)   *Is he accessible?*

(iii)   *Will the person be willing at all to honour the invitation?*

(iv)   *Is he likely to co-operate fully with the exercise?*

(v)   *How are we going to get a person who showed an unco-operative attitude in the earlier interrogation to honour our invitation and so on?*

This is one of the basic reasons why in the conduct of all interrogation, the interrogator must always exhibit the highest professional standards possible so that he does not create an unnecessary buffer for himself; he must constantly ensure due diligence for the *respect of the human rights* of every person he encounters. Such professional attitude can lay a good foundation for co-operation whenever that becomes necessary.

Now, we need to take special note that every invitation in respect of a Confrontation should be strictly on individual basis and should be under a *very good cover*. That means the investigator has to invite each person without letting the other party or parties involved or any other third person know of it. Each person so invited should not under any circumstance be made to know or even suspect the least that there is going to be a Confrontation of any sort. We may invite the person to help us solve a personal problem, for instance, or use some other good cover. In this case we shall emphasize that *because the invitation is to help the interrogator solve a purely private problem, we do not want anyone to hear about it, etc.* In doing this, we <u>ensure</u> that we let the fellow feel very <u>recognized</u> and <u>respected</u>.

(b) ***Timing:*** Enquire about when a person can honour our invitation, if our proposed time is not suitable. *We do not order the fellow to appear before us.* This is not a Law Court where one can be subpoenaed. It is always advisable to first work out the time with the person more likely to be difficult or known to be difficult and then try to convince the others to accept that. The situation is easier when the persons to be drafted for the Confrontation are in Custody as seen earlier. The interrogator must ensure that all the persons so invited are available to him for the exercise at the scheduled or agreed time. He must also ensure the he is very punctual himself. Where and when facilities permit, it is ideal to receive each invitee at a separate room prior to the exercise so that one party is not made aware of the presence of the other, as they arrive one after the other, until the exercise itself is set to commence or commences.

(c) **_Purpose:_** Remember that the actual purpose of an invitation is never disclosed to any of the persons so invited or who would be needed at the "Confrontation". This is only let out when all the various persons invited for the Confrontation have been Assembled before the Interrogator(s) and everything is set for the commencement of the exercise. Gently let all the parties appreciate the importance of the Confrontation, especially in view of their respective involvement in the case. It should be made very clear to them that none of them was before a Court at that sitting but that interrogators were only interested in fairness, objectivity and truth in respect of the case on hand so that the results or findings will be very clear and 'helpful' to everybody.

(d) **_Venue:_** The Venue for a Confrontation needs to be exclusively convenient for the purpose. The interrogator needs to select a place that will not suffer _distraction_ and _intrusion_ just as the initial interrogation. _It is woefully UNPROFESSIONAL OR INAPPROPRIATE TO USE CONGESTED OFFICES_ to organize a Confrontation. Where and when Officers normally sit in Congested Offices, one such offices may be set aside, when need be, within a particular period during normal working hours for the purpose but of course with permission from Superior Officers; otherwise, the exercise can be organized outside normal working hours.

(e) **_Security:_** Just as in all interrogation the security of the exercise and the individual participants is paramount, so it is also in the case of _Confrontation._ It must be explained further that when we talk of "Security" in a Confrontation, we are not referring only to the invitational aspect. We are also concerned about how secured the SPECIFIC as well as the GENERAL ENVIRONMENT of the exercise is throughout the Confrontation.

(f) ___Independent Witness___: It is required in interrogation involving criminal cases especially, that an Independent Witness be present throughout. Therefore, while arranging to hold a Confrontation, the interrogator needs to ensure that at least he secures two Independent Witnesses for the exercise. In case one disappoints, the other will be available.

(g) ___Interpreters:___ These would be required just as at the main or initial interrogation. The same people used in the initial interrogation would be preferred for continuity and security reasons, unless they did not perform well in the initial interrogation.

IMPORTANCE OF CONFRONTATION

You will agree that the importance of interrogation is to establish the TRUTH or TRUE FACTS about an allegation or an uncertainty for decision making such as Judgements or Correct Prescription of Charges against suspects and accused. On a larger platform, they are needed for Policy Formulation and this cuts across all facets of the economy of a State.

So, where facts are not well established, the consequence is immense. It could lead to dismissals of innocent people, imprisonment of poor, innocent and helpless people and in fact various other forms of victimization which ultimately tend to adversely affect the socio-economic development of a country. Workers can, for instance, go on strike just for three days over the 'wrongful dismissal' of a colleague and three days of such industrial action can get the economy of any State on its knees.

State Security could be gravely jeopardized, also, when true facts about security-related

Issues are not well-established. Wrong security measures could be applied to vital situations such that at the end of the day *a particular security problem would rather keep recurring and/or compounding instead of being checked.* National Economic issues are no exception in this regard.

These are a few of the reasons why in situations where there is the need to clarify issues, the interrogator or investigator should not hesitate to do just that; and 'Confrontation' is one vital means of doing that, subject to circumstances of a specific case, and should therefore not be ignored where and when it becomes necessary.

DEGREES OF INTERROGATION

1. First Degree Interrogation:

This is the normal, most widely used and most acceptable form of interrogation. Under this kind, no form of force or threat is applied to anyone whatsoever throughout the interrogation. In an era of growing global democratization and practice of the rule of law, it is advisable for an interrogator not to apply any kind of force or threat to anyone brought in for interrogation. In other words, no form of force or threat should be applied on anyone to be interrogated before, during and after such an exercise.

Admittedly, there happen to be situations when persons being interrogated:

1. Refuse to talk; or

2. Show unprovoked arrogance to the interrogator (usually calculated to achieve an aim); or

3. Refuse to provide vital evidence or information to which they clearly have access or know about, etc.

Such situations should not necessitate the use of force or threat on anyone under interrogation. *This Book does not encourage the use of force, threat or intimidation in interrogation.* Patience, good strategies and common sense can do the trick.

The story is told of a certain country battling with terrorist attacks all round its jurisdictions world-wide, and whose security officers (not all, of course) mainly use severe torture to interrogate persons suspected of involvement in terror acts against her.

The highly inhumane methods used by these officers to compel information or "false evidence" from high-profile suspects during interrogation unfortunately never succeeded to deliver useful results. Such methods did not yield any life-saving information to that country's security systems.

Many of its citizens of very high repute spoke against the practice, yet, all that fell on deaf ears. The obvious result was that the country's security risks were highly aggravated both internally and externally.

Here, one can easily appreciate the **REAL DEPTH OF DANGER associated with non-compliance to basic principles in interrogation in relation to contemporary global trends and rather doing one's own thing.** This buttresses the position of this book not being in favour of any form of force, threat or intimidation in the conduct of interrogation. Now one sees clearly the ALL-TIME problem that just a few interrogators have created for the government of that country globally.

We can conclude here that it is helpful to always operate within existing laws and also respect the human rights of suspects. Any slip can be very fatal.

2. Second Degree Interrogation

In this form of interrogation, the interrogator applies a reasonable amount of force on the person being interrogated to compel him to voice out some needed information or to accept responsibility for a crime/offence for which he is suspected of involvement.

The phony thing about this kind of system is that *there is no means to measure or determine the exact limits of such 'reasonable' use of force.* Oh, yes!! How can you determine the limits of force or brutality that can be applied on a suspect or accused to compel him to 'provide' evidence in a case he is suspected of involvement. Virtually, most Officers who use this method end up rather applying The Third Degree Interrogation, if care is not taken, and this is a very, very, very risky thing to do.

3. Third Degree Interrogation

In this type, all manner of brutality are applied on a suspect, accused and sometimes even on witnesses. It could be applied before, during or after interrogation. Some Officers sometimes use persons who are not part of the interrogation to carry out such atrocities. It is a very dangerous and crude way of interrogating someone. It can easily land the investigator in big trouble!!

Such brutalities may involve the application of Threats, Pain, Debilitation, Disorientation and Deprivation.

Threats: The objective here is for interrogators to create terror or the belief that an unbearable and undesirable event is in the offing for the suspect concerned. Threats mainly work on fear or anticipated pain.

Pain: This is a basic technique and may involve physical beatings, use of instruments of torture, etc.

Debilitation: This has to do with the systematic weakening of a suspect physically or psychologically. Physically, it may involve physical drills especially in the hot sun, in a torrential rain, carrying of very heavy loads, etc. Psychologically, a suspect may be subjected to extreme humiliation like striping him/her naked in the open, forced religious practices, mock executions, etc.

Disorientation: The strategy here is to play down on the suspect's sense of judgement and the ability to make rational decisions. It may involve the use of narcotics, hypnotics, rapid barrage of questions, etc.

Deprivation: This has to do with denying a suspect of basic needs that can lead to pain or desperation. That includes extreme hunger and/or thirst, denial of sleep, solitary confinement for long periods, etc.

All these, and many more, are aimed at subjecting suspects to fear and unbearable pain to compel them to make *confessions badly needed by interrogators* at a given time or in a given situation. It however needs to be noted carefully that certain hardened criminals like terrorists, drug barons and coup plotters can be immune to threats and pain. Above all, such forced confessions may not necessarily stand the test of time as seen earlier in the example involving the CIA in the United States of America that we have just considered.

Now, supposing during a brutalization, in the name of interrogation, a person dies, what would the interrogator achieve? And what would he do? These are very big questions! You would lose all the information you are seeking from the person and in addition be charged with a criminal offence (murder)for which you do not even qualify for a bail. Just imagine! Some investigators who use this rather crude method of interrogation normally wrongly consider themselves as being the more experienced or experts in the trade. But, they lie. They are living in a fool's paradise. We need to be nice to everybody at all times and apply professional principles rather *very responsibly*; for, Principles are principles, but common sense must always be applied to make them more meaningful. This is the position of this Book as a training material for very responsible Officers.

Now, since an interrogator cannot tell the exact physical or health condition (*and if you like, spiritual condition*) of a suspect at any point in time, it is advisable not to use any kind of force, threat or intimidation during interrogation. We saw earlier in this Book how the interrogator needed to always weigh SUCCESS against RISK, with this author citing two real cases involving himself. He indicated that the higher the RISK, the less SUCCESS is likely.

THE INTERROGATION REPORT

An *Interrogation Report* does not represent a full Investigation Report. Interrogation is part of Investigation as much as Criminal Cases are concerned.

Some Committees Of Enquiry, as well as Investigators, have not lived up to expectation and have done more harm than good in their Reports because they have used *Interrogation Reports* in place of INVESTIGATION REPORTS, perhaps ignorantly, for the benefit of the doubt.

In serious fact finding exercises, questioning suspects, accused or witnesses alone does not conclude investigations. Sometimes even ordinary witnesses can turn real or principal suspects, if one gets a little beyond interrogation to conduct thorough checks elsewhere to support the findings of an interrogation.

It is very needful, therefore, to conduct field checks even with certain answers provided by suspects, accused or witnesses at an interrogation to ascertain the truth before coming up with a comprehensive useful Report. Don't forget that the overall aim of interrogation is to establish the extent of involvement, or non-involvement, of suspects, accused or witnesses in a crime or an offence, and this must always be thoroughly done.

Done with the above introduction, let us now proceed to look at the format for a typical Interrogation Report. This is not the same as a Statement taken from a suspect, accused or witness. The *Interrogation Report* is made up of special notes taken down by the interrogator from the answers provided by the suspect, accused or witness at each session of interrogation. It must be devoid of any personal emotions, bias or other prejudices.

Unlike a Statement, the exact *content* of an Interrogation Report is not known by the suspect, accused or witness *(See the Chapter on Statements)*. This is so because, at least, certain critical observations made and/or discerned by means of various *Interrogation Techniques* are contained in the Interrogation Report, and that cannot be disclosed to the suspect, accused or witness for any reason. If the mannerism of a suspect, accused or witness clearly betrayed him during interrogation, such an observation cannot under any circumstance be disclosed to the suspect, accused or witness for any reason, for instance.

On its part, a *Statement* is written by the suspect, accused or witness or any other person required to do so for various reasons. It may also be written on their behalf by persons appointed by them after which they themselves will acknowledge, procedurally, as being their true Statement.

The *Interrogation Report* is different. It is written by the Interrogator himself. The Statement from the suspect, accused or witness goes with The Interrogation Report as an *Attachment*. It is a COMPONENT of the Interrogation Report. *An INVESTIGATION REPORT* embodies the Interrogation Report – plus its Attached Fully Written Statement by suspect, accused, or witness AND findings obtained from crime scenes, searches, elicitation, bills, publications, surveillance, and various other sources of information, by the investigator. So, a Statement, an Interrogation Report and an Investigation Report are never the same.

Now, our concern here is not for a full Investigation Report. We are looking at a situation where a *Separate Interrogation Report* has to be written. What should it entail and how might it be presented, among others. We cannot run away from the fact that there are several situations where the same 'occurrence, event or case' is referred to about three equally competent State Investigative Organizations to investigate. This is real; and it is because of MISTRUST, even at that high level! Who knows what aspect who is handling? It is also possible that as one State Investigative Organization is tasked with Secret Investigation into a case; another, at the same time, can also be made to just interrogate the suspects and report (Open Investigation). Two independent Reports would be submitted from different State Organizations: One might be *an Interrogation Report* and the other *a Surveillance Report or Normal Investigation Report*. Such a situation, would normally bring up very hard facts or truths that can hardly be disputed if and only if the two Reports are diligently prepared, compared and combined.

The following are essential in an Interrogation Report:

INTERROGATION REPORT

REF. NO:_____

CLASSIFICATION: *Secret.*

ORIGINATOR:_____

RECIPIENT:_____

PRIORITY:_____

PANEL MEMBERS:_____

   1. TITLE OF REPORT: (Case):_____

   2. DATE(S) OF INTERROGATION: (Not Report):_____

   3. SESSIONS: (1ʳᵗ, 2ⁿᵈ, 3ʳᵈ, etc)_____

   4. TIME: (a)Start_____ (b)Closed_____ (c)Duration:_____

   5. PLACE (Venue for each session, specify):_____

   _____

   6. FULL NAME *{Accused/Suspect/Witness}*:_____

   7. PERMANENT ADDRESS*{Accused/Suspect/Witness}*_____

   _____

   8. (a) PROFESSION:_____

      (b) OCCUPATION:_____

   9. INCIDENT/NOTABLE EVENT(if any, during interrogation).

E.g. *Attempted escape from custody, hospitalization of accused/suspect/ witness; unprovoked violent behaviour of suspect/accused/witness*

_____

_____

10. SEISMIC/METEOROLOGICAL CONDITION(during interrogation): e.g. *earthquake, heavy rainstorm, volcanic eruption, normal weather:*_____ {any of these and other weather conditions can affect an interrogation exercise in diverse ways and must be reported}.

11. ANY CONSTRAINTS (*at each session*):_____

12. DETAILS: (Accurate Record of findings/notes taken at the interrogation):_____

_____

_____

_____etc.

13. COMMENTS/OBSERVATION (e.g. could not be implicated, *justification*; could be implicated, *justification*; etc)_____

_____

_____

_____

14. RECOMMENDATION (e.g. whether witness should be held as a suspect; whether need to organize a 'Confrontation'; whether need to do further interrogation; etc).

15. SIGNATURE: (Principal Interrogator/Chairman of Committee Of Enquiry etc)_____

16. DATE (Of Interrogation Report).

NOTES:

The interrogator should not be judgemental <u>even if in his view and from the facts obtained from the interrogation a suspect is clearly guilty of the offence for which the exercise was ordered.</u>

Supposing by normal human error the Report gets leaked, for sure the Interrogator stands to be blamed by the "guilty" faction and in some situations attacked by any means (physically, or by ordeal, according to the culture of the operative environment).

Also, other investigative findings might prove certain aspects of the Interrogation Report to be just half-truths or simply unjustifiable. There could be many dire consequences.

The Investigator can express his individual opinion in the analysis/ comments section of the Report and the expressions commonly used include: *"...it could be..."; or "...could have...", and such likes, as in:*

1. It *could be* that suspect King Kong actually committed the murder.

2. Suspect King Kong *could not have* or *may not have* actually committed the murder, from the facts obtained in the interrogation.

3. It *might be possible* that King Kong committed the murder, in view of the facts adduced from the interrogation.

Such expressions only indicate, in clear terms, one's OPINION and not ACCUSATIVE.

It is preferred that the final decision of guilt or otherwise be left with higher or final authorities in the appropriate Organization, the Judiciary or the Rightful Consumer of the Report, (i.e. the one who called for the investigation or interrogation to be conducted, say, The Office Of The President, The Minister Of Health, The Vice Chancellor, etc).

Furthermore, emotions should not be introduced into the Report. *It has the potential to mislead one to make a wrong assessment or analyses of the facts available or obtained.* Usually emotions in such situations are triggered by passion, bias or prejudice. One needs to guard against these tendencies.

Finally, specific incidents that took place during the exercise and that impacted on the smooth conduct of the interrogation, if any, need to be reported; for instance, *very frequent request to attend nature's call by a particular suspect or witness; sudden ill health/hospitalization of a suspect or witness or interrogator and so on; AND FOR ALL THAT,* what was the response of the interrogators? For instance, in the case of sickness, the interrogator must state clearly whether the suspect was taken to hospital, or the interrogator administered drugs to him. And if so, what were the *time in* and *time out, by who and by what means - air, road, bicycles, car, ambulance or on foot, etc.*

[Administering drugs to suspects this way should always be avoided due to the dangers associated with it. A certified health professional must be made to do that and appropriate records kept on that.]

It is therefore obligatory, on the part of the interrogator, to follow the right procedures always in order not to infringe on anyone's rights and lose a good case in Court, when that becomes necessary.

CHAPTER 5

ARRESTS, SEARCHES AND DETENTION

<u>ARRESTS</u>

When it comes to 'Arrests', the first thing that must strike the investigator is:

(a) Is there any need at all to effect any arrest?". If yes, then,

(b) What is the justification for that decision?

Arrests can be made when:

(i)   One is found in the act of committing an offence;

(ii)   When there is sufficient grounds to believe that a person intends to commit a crime;

(iii)   A person has committed a crime or has earlier been declared wanted by a competent jurisdiction like the Police, the Law Courts or other State Institution that has such rights;

(iv)   There is sufficient grounds to believe that a person (or group) is about to commit a crime or offence.

(v)   There is sufficient grounds to believe that a person assisted in one way or the other in a criminal activity.

(vi)   There is sufficient grounds to believe that a person benefited from a criminal activity.

Again, where and when there is enough justification for arrest, many issues must be cleared before setting out to arrest any suspect. These include:

(i)   How urgent is it to effect the arrest of a suspect?" This depends on the gravity of the offence allegedly committed, being committed (not necessarily in the presence of the arresting Officer) or about to be committed by that suspect, his 'presumed' extent of involvement in the case, and the unlikelihood of the suspect readily making himself available as and when needed by investigators/prosecutors in respect of the case in contention.

(ii)   What is the most ***Operationally Convenient place*** to effect a suspect's arrest?" Arrests are usually quiet, peaceful, easy and smooth. Take note that this is not the case all the time. It depends largely on the calibre of the criminal/suspect in question, the level of professionalism of the Investigator and the hostile nature of the environment where the suspect is located and how the suspect is hailed there.

(iii)   The calibre of person(s) held as suspect(s) in relation to the magnitude of the offence and 'as the culture of the operative environment dictates'.

(iv)   The level of a suspect's security consciousness as well as the physical security structures surrounding the suspect. Does he go with strong body guards? Is he always armed with deadly weapons? How about carnivals in his home or office and so on?

Note: The **personal safety** of the investigator **must never be compromised** under any circumstance for the "success" of an investigation. There must always be a **reasonable balance** between RISK and SUCCESS as much as investigation is concerned. The higher the Risk, the lower the chances of Success. This is inevitable. And, the lower the risk, the higher the chances of success. This is quite obvious.

As much as possible, violence should be avoided in effecting any arrest. Life is most precious. This Book, nevertheless, concurs with the application of reasonable force in effecting arrests, especially when an attempt is made by suspects to resist arrest or to go on the offensive without provocation. Self-Defence, when the need arises, is obviously a "no compromise" in circumstances of this nature. What this book is saying, in effect, is that in all such possibilities, *__one must always ensure that there is enough justification to act the manner he wants to or choses, and that the investigator's life should never be sacrificed for the success of an investigation.__*

Let's share this experience:

It happened on a cool afternoon when this writer and a colleague investigator had spent weeks monitoring a very dangerous Senior Military Officer (who was then deemed a threat to State Security) and had sufficiently closed in on him (the Military Officer) for his arrest. The Army Officer inadvertently entered a major Military Barracks. Even though these two investigators mustered courage and also entered the Camp, they did not pursue their agenda, except to clandestinely take special note of "certain peculiarities" for purposes of informing 'Base' about developments.

These two investigators, in view of the prevailing atmosphere that cannot certainly be depicted on this platform, were to choose between RISK and SUCCESS in a matter of moments - not even seconds: BUT, just moments! They benefited from Divine providence instantly and settled for their safety first; and success and 'fame' had no place here. They immediately reported accurately on all events. What a scenario to recall!! You might want to know at this juncture 'what happened to these investigators'.

And, YES, if anyone cares to know what happened to them, the answer is: NOTHING WAS DONE TO THEM. Why? Because their Superiors were Real Professionals themselves and perfectly understood their Report far better than the originators themselves. And so must it be always.

CAUTION: *Let no one read this piece and, when given genuine assignments by his Superiors, will decide to "do his own thing". That will certainly backfire with time. There is always One Truth in every situation. When you are able to declare it, that is the end. It is sealed for ever.*

Not too long ago, a Senior Security Officer (SSO) had to command an exercise for the tracking down of an armed robber who had successfully lured a Businessman from a far away country. The businessman arrived in the host country with a substantial amount of hard currency and the armed robber was trying to lure this man into an isolated place or hotel to snatch the money from him.

After two days of constant monitoring, even in the nights, and "controlling of events", the final episode was staged at an open air restaurant about three minutes drive from the only International Airport of the that host country. The Armed Robber had agreed on mobile phone, a few hours earlier that same afternoon, finally, to meet the businessman at that very spot, and the former did actually turn up around 4.00pm.

Under the command of the SSO, the businessman was carefully positioned (or made to sit at a special spot at the restaurant) for operational reasons. Some Immigration Officers, mostly in plain clothes, who had been roped in for assistance, were also well positioned. The necessary operational arrangements were all made inside the airport itself. Request for armed Police Assistance far earlier from the Divisional Command of the local Police was however politely turned down on grounds of "no personnel"; but, the exercise had to be conducted.

Eventually, the SSO, per special means, spotted the armed robber in question in black suit, with two body guards entering the Departure Hall, without luggage, and surprisingly with very cheeky ease in the full glare of security details posted at that entrance. After about thirty minutes he came out of the Departure Hall by the same route with his two guards and strolled straight to the Restaurant in question.

In a nutshell, the armed robber came and took a position at a distance of about twenty meters from that of the Businessman at the Restaurant, having obtained a physical description of the Businessman on phone earlier; and he immediately ordered for meat (khebab) and drinks. The SSO also took a "careful position" for effective monitoring and in the process quietly noticed that certain suspicious individuals were coming in one after another and who communicated by 'silent' signals with the 'suspected armed robber'. Twenty two (22) of them, including a woman, were identified in that group.

In very cautious turns, two of them joined the table of the suspected robber and his two body guards. After about thirty (30) minutes of 'copious' boozing and profuse smoking, which suddenly changed the atmosphere at the restaurant, these began to visit the washroom in turns of about five minutes intervals. That alone made them out. The staff over there grouped suddenly inside a room at the restaurant and consulted briefly. They had obviously sensed real danger.

Furthermore, the SSO was well positioned to hear each person who passed into the washroom load a weapon there. After the third such experience, he had no other option than to take very swift measures to COMPROMISE THE **SUCCESS** OF THE EXERCISE FOR THE **SAFETY** OF THE ENTIRE *OPERATIONAL TEAM AND THE BUSINESSMAN WITH HIS MONEY. In a matter of moments, the* businessman was taken out of the area into a very secured place and the Operational Team also received appropriate signals to take cover since real danger was imminent. The exercise was altogether called off, even though its success, after two days of monitoring, was in sight; but, NOT IN THE FULL GLARE OF IMMINENT DANGER!

The Operational Team would have erred if they had allowed these twenty-two Armed Robbers at that moment to snatch the businessman's money before trying to use force to apprehend them; that would have certainly resulted in fatalities and eventually the businessman losing his money. Hence, the need to swiftly call off the entire operation and save lives and money.

This is another instance where and when SAFETY must never be compromised for SUCCESS!!

(v)   The TIME to effect arrest is also important and here we consider:

(a) What time of the year, month, week, day or hour of the day is most suitable for a successful arrest of a suspect. These strategies should of course be in relation to the personal security consciousness of the suspect in his daily movements as well as the physical security arrangement in his proximal and distant environments. The TIME to effect a person's arrest is normally informed by a good knowledge of his habits and associates: what time does he leave for work and return home? What time does he reach the office and leave there? Which routes does he often take? Which places or restaurants does he often visit and how long does he often stay there? Is he normally armed with dangerous weapons? Is he normally accompanied by strong body guards? and so on.

(b) The weather on a particular day and at a particular place can sometimes strategically influence a successful arrest.

Consider this further : *On January 8, 1997, the Meteorological Services Department (MSD) announced on Radio and Television early in the morning that a very heavy storm was going to sweep through the town of Saviet and its surrounding towns and villages between the hours of 6.05am and 12 noon. The duration of the active storm was not given. The announcement, however, cautioned the general public against the enormity of the storm and asked all to stay indoors and that drivers should also park their vehicles during the storm.*

Interestingly, investigators took advantage of this weather condition, mounted surveillance on a very slippery suspect that they had struggled to arrest for some time and arrested

him just before the storm went into full flight, a time when
everybody had taken cover against the storm.

This is an instance when the weather can positively impact on an arrest.

But, every coin has two sides. Investigators went to a town to arrest a suspect and on reaching the place there was a heavy downpour that lasted several hours, even eating into the next day and resulting in deadly floods all over the vast area; the floods in fact sent everybody, including animals, running in all directions for their lives; the investigators themselves no exception. What would happen? The 'Operation' would not be successful, simply put.

The actual point being made here is that the weather condition for an area in any particular day or period of the day, can influence an operation and needs to be carefully considered, *but not ignored during investigations.* So then, before investigators set out to conduct arrests on any particular day, they need to be abreast with the weather condition/forecast for that day. That can even inform them as to what type of protective costume they will need to go out with.

MASS ARRESTS (SWOOPS)

Mass arrests or swoops sometimes appear to be the only option left to apprehend "suspects" or criminals or wanted persons identified to be living or hiding in a particular locality or suburb. But, just as every coin has two sides, this system may not be justified or helpful in every situation.

Consider the following Report:

"Ninety-nine suspected commercial sex workers and thieves have been arrested
in a police swoop carried out early this morning, 5/2/2005, at Asemsebe, in
the Eastern Region.

The suspects were forty-two females alleged to be commercial sex workers and the rest, all males, suspected to be pick-pockets, mobile phone snatchers and armed robbers. Those arrested were between the ages of 10 and 38 and were picked up at drinking spots, a brothel and a market. Three other persons were also arrested for operating brothels which accommodated some of the suspects. Items found on them included shoes, mobile phones, clothes and condoms."

Be it as it may, this Report brings up very interesting issues.

(i)   What was the objective for conducting this exercise at all?

(ii)   Was the method used the best?

(iii)   Was that the only option to achieve that objective?

(iv)   Was the 'objective' actually achieved?

(v)   Can the suspects be truly prosecuted or given a fair trial?

(vi)   Will the Police be able to thoroughly interrogate each of the suspects, as required by law, and obtain their individual statements?

The answers to these simple questions to justify the action of the Police can only be far-fetched. The evidence available in the report is clearly not strong enough for any honest Judge to convict them.

There might be a laudable objective of "ridding society of bad elements". That is good. The method used cannot however be justifiable for all the "suspects". How can the Police tell whether or not some of the persons swooped are just on family visits or on some decent mission and have only been caught up in the swoop as "criminals" and worse still even put up in the news. Truly, some of the victims might be on family visits; others might also just be passers-by and so on.

Now, one would wonder how the Police can thoroughly interrogate all ninety-nine (99) "suspects" in a week or so and prepare them for prosecution. Convicting en-masse this way obviously infringes on the human rights of such "suspects" because each of them must be told his specific offence for which he or she is being held, and which the Police MUST PROVE BEYOND REASONABLE DOUBTS. Besides, each of the "suspects" so being held by the Police MUST, by law, be given a fair chance to explain himself or herself at an interrogation. Then, at prosecution, is each suspect MUST again be provided access to Counsel of his or her OWN CHOICE, as mandated by law. Many of them might be denied fair trials and end up languishing in jails for many years unlawfully; others might be forgotten as remand prisoners for years unjustifiably and many other very unfortunate situations can ensue.

Rhetorically, *Why is it that swoops are mostly, if not always, conducted on poor helpless people in society? Can they be the only "deadly criminals" around?*

The conviction of this book is that "ALL ARRESTS MUST BE JUSTIFIABLE SO THAT THE RIGHTS OF INDIVIDUALS ARE NOT VIOLATED AT WILL".

We may take note of the following Criminal Procedures:

(a) Upon arrest, let the suspect know, immediately, why he is under arrest, as required by law. We cannot just bundle someone anyhow and send him to detention. He has the right to know why he is under arrest and why he has to be detained.

(b) Let the suspect know his right to counsel of his own choice in respect of his arrest and detention or the case in which he is suspected of involvement.

(c) Every arrest must be reported immediately to the next higher authority (in an Organisation) or to the appropriate State Security Establishment, e.g. Police, Immigration, Customs, Military, as the case may require.

(d) Suspect's 'pictures' must be taken immediately after arrest, with or without suspect's consent as circumstances permit; in case of escape, for instance, that can conveniently be published for a possible re-arrest. The pictures must be taken from different dimensions and "object distances".

(e) Finger-prints of all ten fingers (or all available fingers, as the case may be), and suspect's height, must also be taken very quickly after the arrest of a suspect.

SEARCH

There are two types of Search, namely:

(i)   Secret Search and

(ii)   Open Search.

Secret Search refers to the clandestine intrusion of a suspect's (or accused's) premises. It is carried out at a **high speed** and **risk.** The specific guiding principles are not discussed in this book for State security reasons. But, basically, one must ensure that nothing is done to create the least suspicion that a secret search has taken place.

Open Search is the normal search common to everyone. It is normally used during or immediately after arrest in the presence of the suspect or accused concerned as well as an Independent Witness. *{See Secret Search in Chapter 1}.* Below are some Criminal Procedures relating to Search:

(a) When one is arrested, his physical body must be thoroughly searched immediately for any evidence and offensive materials/ objects which could be used to cause harm.

(b) As much as possible, involve an Independent Witness in all searches. This is however not applicable to Secret Search which has its own principles.

(c) The premises of the criminal or suspect must be thoroughly searched also without delay; i.e. his houses, his cars, offices, shops etc. (This, of course, includes other relevant places associated with the suspect where evidence could be obtained).

(d) During a search, the Date, Time, Place, Particulars of Witnesses present, as well as all relevant items found must be ***instantly, accurately and distinctly recorded*** in the presence of the suspect who must jointly endorse, appropriately, the inventory so taken, with the witnesses present. This is not referring to "Secret Search" which has its own principles.

(e) Always take very swift measures to cordon off or protect the scene of crime/offence in order to preserve evidence there. Whether or not the place cannot be searched immediately, always get very neat video or other very clear photographic recording of the entire affected crime scene instantly. Ensure physical protection of the crime scene up to a reasonable time when all relevant evidence must have been sufficiently lifted by investigators.

(f) All body searches must be done with utmost decency. A female Officer must search a female suspect and a male must search a male suspect. This rule is **not negotiable** in investigation.

DETENTION : Suspects or Accused Persons are held behind bars for various reasons and under different conditions subject to the discretion of the Case Officer, Prosecutor or Judge AND existing legislation. Sometimes people are detained over a very limited time solely for their own safety from reprisal attacks. Detention can also be determined in relation to the status of the suspect or accused, the nature/gravity of the offence in contention, the criminal records of the suspect/accused and social/political influences.

The availability of GOOD DETENTION FACILITIES is paramount. Even that, is there any need to detain a suspect at all, in the first place? We detain when there is absolutely the need to do so (*See the notes below*).

Fancy the nearest detention facility available to an investigator has only one room (cell) for all suspects. How do we cope with say two females and three males arrested for the same crime or offence in the same cell either; else it will be very easy for them to strategize to outwit interrogators, let alone combining female and male suspects in a common cell. That would be quite outrageous. The proximity of the available detention facility from the investigator or interrogation centre is also very important. Then also, how do we provide the necessary security for each of the suspects so arrested for possible detention? Is there any need to keep a particular suspect reasonably far away from the Operational Centre and so on? Such issues need quick and very careful consideration or anticipation at the planning stage for a successful exercise.

The following need to be noted carefully in respect of detention:

(a) Always keep within existing legislation. This must not be compromised under any circumstance or for any reason.

(b) Ensure all efforts to grant bail to the suspect or offender have not proved practicable and that the fault cannot be deliberate on the part of the Case Officer, or his Organization.

(c) Ensure the person to be detained is in good health, or else seek the necessary medical attention from a State-recognized competent health facility before keeping him behind bars. See to it, promptly, that appropriate and accurate records are kept on all such arrangements, especially in the Station Diary. Extracts should also be quickly served on appropriate higher authorities. Such sick suspects/accused should be monitored at REGULAR VERY SHORT INTERVALS in the cells and accurate records kept for the attention of superior officers.

(d) A Diary of Action must equally be kept on all these events accurately.

(e) Ensure that weapons and other substances or objects that can be injurious to any of the inmates or that can aid a jail break are not permitted into the cells.

(f) Ensure very regular visits (at short but varied intervals) to the cells and accurate records promptly kept on all observations, suspicions, and so on, for the attention of superior officers.

But, let me quickly stress here that the need to effect an arrest cannot be constrained by the availability of detention facilities. Arrests are carried out if and only if there are enough justification for that. We do not say we will not arrest armed robbers any longer because we do not have enough good detention facilities. That will be a very big goof!!

That done, we then consider HOW the arrest has to be made in an efficient professional manner. Will that be by clandestine means or otherwise. Then also, how ready are we, after a successful arrest, to conduct a perfect or neat search on the suspects so arrested. What type of searches will be more appropriate under each circumstance and how ready shall we be at the time for the purpose? These are all critical issues requiring due attention.

All the above concern situations where any arrest is yet to be made. But, where and when an arrest has been effected already, the investigator will concern himself mainly with the application of Criminal Procedures involving Arrest, Search and Detention.

In the case of Detention, again, Criminal Procedures require that always one must ensure:

(i) To keep within existing legislation;

(ii) All efforts to grant bail to the suspect or offender have not proved practicable and that the fault cannot be deliberate on the part of the Case Officer, or his Organisation.

(iii) The person to be detained is in good health, or else seek the necessary medical attention from a State-recognized competent health facility before anyone is detained. Ensure appropriate and accurate records are kept on all such arrangements, especially in the Station Diary. Extracts should also be sent to appropriate higher authorities immediately. A Diary Of Action must equally be kept on all these events. Such sick suspects should be monitored at REGULAR SHORT INTERVALS, while in cells, and accurate records kept on all that for the attention of superior officers.

(iv)   Always ensure that weapons and other substances that can be injurious to any of the inmates or that can aid a jail break are not permitted into the cells. Ensure VERY REGULAR VISITS (AT SHORT INTERVALS) TO THE CELLS and promptly keep accurate records on all findings/observation.

CHAPTER 6

STATEMENTS

A *Statement,* in Criminal Investigations, refers to a written account of a specific situation by a person who is involved, suspected of involvement, a witness or one who ordinarily has some useful information to volunteer in respect of an issue under investigation or of interest to an Organization or to State Security.

TYPES OF STATEMENTS

The main types are:

(a) *Cautioned Statements*

(b) *Witness Statements*

(c) *Complainant Statements*

(d) *Voluntary Statements*

(e) *Confession Statements*

(f) *Charged Statements.*

Cautioned Statements

A Cautioned Statement is an extremely important aspect of Criminal Investigations. It is taken from a person who is either suspected of involvement or actually involved in a case under investigation. So, then, in effect, we have two main forms of Cautioned Statements, namely:

1. Accused Cautioned Statement

2. Suspect Cautioned Statement.

The former is taken from a person who is ***accused*** of an offence; the latter is taken from a person ***suspected of involvement*** in an offence or case.

Cautioned *Statements* are always preceded by "Cautioned Words" (or words of caution) that spell out:

(a) *The exact offence or suspected offence;*

(b) *The right of the suspect or accused to willingly make a Statement;*

(c) *The right of the suspect or accused to consult any Counsel (lawyer) of his own choice.*

All other Statements do not necessarily have Cautioned Words. The various Cautioned Words Read as follows:

Suspect Caution Words
*"A case of… (briefly state exact offence or offences here)… in which you are **suspected to be involved** is under investigation. You are not obliged to say anything unless you wish to do so and that whatever you say shall be recorded in writing and same tendered in evidence against you. You are entitled to Counsel of your own choice."*

Accused Caution Words
*"A case of… (clearly quote the exact Charge here)… in which you are **involved** is under investigation. You are not obliged to say anything unless you wish to do so and that whatever you say shall be recorded and same tendered in evidence against you. You are entitled to Counsel of your own choice."*

We shall look at these again when we come to "Writing A Statement" later in this Chapter.

Witness Statement

This type is usually that which is given by a person who is not involved in a case but has a proof of it.

Complainant Statement

As the name implies, this is the usual Statement taken from a person who makes a complaint to an Organization usually with the intention of seeking legal redress.

Voluntary Statement

This is the Statement made by a person "without necessarily being invited to do so". It is normally made by a person who has not committed any offence but is on his own volition providing information to an Organization usually to help solve an issue not necessarily of personal interest to him.

Confession Statement

This type is similar to a voluntary statement but not the same. It is that which is willingly made by a person to voluntarily admit his involvement in a case.

Charged Statement

This is the Statement made by a person whose involvement in a case is established and subsequently charged for the specific crime. (See Accused Cautioned Statement).

HOW TO OBTAIN STATEMENTS

Statements are normally taken (written) on Statement Forms. (*See Appendix A at the end of this Book*).

But, before we look at Statement Writing itself, it must be noted that before taking a Statement from someone, the investigator must first carefully interrogate the person along the lines of the requirements of the specific case under investigation. This must be done in the most friendly atmosphere possible.

It must equally be noted, furthermore, that a Statement can be taken from a person only when he is willing to do so out of his own free-will. Force should never be applied.

Then also it is not advisable to take a Statement from a seriously sick person or one who complains of any other serious natural discomfort such as hunger, thirst, etc unless the person himself is willing to make such a Statement under such conditions. Among other reasons, a person in any such condition may lose focus in the course of making a Statement and he may deny certain facts in his own certified true Statement, later.

Finally, always ensure an Independent Witness is present before taking a Statement from someone, no matter what type of Statement is involved.

With these few basics noted, let us now proceed to look at *The Statement Form*, the paper on which the Statement is written.

THE STATEMENT FORM

In Criminal Investigations, Statements are taken on *Statement Forms* specially designed for the purpose. A typical Statement Form has three (3) main parts.

The first part is found on the top right corner of the first page of the Statement Form. It comprises "SECTION, STATION, and DATE".

All are to be completed by the investigator (usually in red ink, but not a fast rule).

The second part is to be completed by the person making the Statement, or on his behalf. It comprises NAME, ADDRESS, OCCUPATION and other personal data on the person making the Statement. Note that this second part varies from Organization to Organization.

The third and last part of the Statement Form comprises sufficient space of horizontally ruled lines, or spaces, where the actual Statement, including the administration of the Caution Words together with their respective Acknowledgement, is written and signed. (*See Appendix A at the end of this Book*).

WRITING A STATEMENT

For an ordinary Statement, one can go ahead straightaway to write the Statement after completing the personal data portion on the Statement Form and ***granted that the person making the Statement has been duly interrogated.***

In the case of Cautioned Statements, the "Caution Words" are administered first verbally to the suspect or accused in a language that he understands very well before same is written on the Statement Form, or vice versa; i.e.

*"A case of …(briefly state the **suspected offence or offences** here)…in which you are suspected to be involved is under investigation. That you are not obliged to say anything unless you wish to do so and that whatever you say shall be recorded in writing and same tendered in evidence against you. You are entitled to Counsel of your own choice."*

OR

*"A case of …(quote the **exact offence or offences** here)…in which you are involved is under investigation. That you are not obliged to say anything unless*

114

you wish to do so and that whatever you say shall be recorded in writing and same tendered in evidence against you. You are entitled to Counsel of your own choice."

That done, and before writing the actual Statement, the suspect or accused will then acknowledge the Caution Words as follows:

"Acknowledgement (Suspect)
I have been told that a case of ...(briefly state the suspected offence or offences here)...in which I am suspected to be involved is under investigation. That I am not obliged to say anything unless I wish to do so and that whatever I say shall be recorded in writing and same tendered in evidence against me. I have also been told of my right to Counsel of my own choice."

OR

Acknowledgement (Accused)
"I have been told that a case of...(quote the exact offence or offences here)... in which I am involved is under investigation. That I am not obliged to say anything unless I wish to do so and that whatever I say shall be recorded in writing and same tendered in evidence against me. I have also been told of my right to Counsel of my own choice."

Both the Caution Words from the investigator and the corresponding Acknowledgement from the suspect or accused must be duly endorsed, with current dates, by the investigator, suspect/accused and the Independent Witness. (*See Appendix B at the end of this Book*).

NOTE: Do not back-date Statements. That can be dangerous.

All that done, the writing of the actual Statement can then follow.

In writing a Statement, generally, the following rules are commonly observed:

1. *There should be no paragraphing;*

2. *Each line of the Statement Form must be fully utilized before going to the next;*

3. *There should be no indecent cancellation; where a mistake is made, it should be neatly crossed through just once and then kept in parenthesis;*

4. *Each page should be clearly numbered (preferably in words) at the top centre;*

5. *The very bottom of every page should be endorsed by the person making the Statement, the investigator and the Independent Witness;*

6. *Where an insertion is made in a Statement, the person making the insertion must sign or initial (with the current date and time of the insertion) against every single insertion;*

7. *Where a person wants to make a Supplementary (additional) Statement, he should be permitted, except that this additional Statement shall not necessarily be on a fresh Statement Form but shall begin immediately on the vacant line after the very end of the previous Statement. It must also be indicated that such an addition is a "Supplementary Statement" and should be endorsed by the person making the Statement, the Investigator and an Independent Witness, with current date and time.*

8. *Where the person making the Statement cannot write his own Statement for various genuine reasons, a competent person can do so for him, but that must strictly be done at the consent of the very person. This, however, should be indicated at the beginning of the Statement as follows, for instance:*

"Suspect/Accused Mark Grennes spoke Swahili and same written down in English on his behalf by …(state the full and correct identity of the person writing the Statement)… as follows: I am Mark Grennes of the Black African Post Office. I am an Engineer by profession and my address is H/No. XLM 452 J, Lapeewa House, # 18 Bully Street, Manners City. I am suspected to be involved, (or accused of involvement, as the case may be) in Fake Passport Deals and wish to make a Statement as follows_____

_____

_____

_____etc.

WRITING A STATEMENT ON BEHALF OF AN ACCUSED, SUSPECT OR WITNESS

In the first place, is it permissible for one to write a Statement for and on behalf of a suspect, an accused or a witness? If yes,

(a) Who qualifies to write such a Statement?

(b) Under what condition is such arrangement legally permissible? And,

(c) How may that be done?

To begin with, we say YES, it is permissible for one to write a Statement for and on behalf of an Accused, a Suspect or Witness but this must be done in the presence of the investigator in charge of the case in question as well as, at least, an Independent Witness.

Sometimes investigators write Statements for and on behalf of accused persons, suspects or witnesses for various reasons as mentioned earlier. That is not bad, BUT, irrespective of how tangible such reasons may be, it is always very necessary for that to be done with the full consent/ approval of the accused, suspect or witness and ensure that **same** consent is accurately recorded on the Statement Form before going ahead to write the actual Statement. All these should be done in the presence of one or two Independent Witnesses, even if the suspect, accused or witness is a close relation or friend of the investigator.

It is better to use at least two Independent Witnesses, under such circumstances, especially in cases involving very serious crimes or hardened criminals.

For instance, supposing an investigator, in writing a Statement for and on behalf of an accused, suspect or witness engages only one Independent Witness and in the prosecution of the very case about two months later in Court, the accused, suspect or witness flatly denies any consent to the writing of his Statement by the Investigator, in spite of any endorsements on the Statement Form by the suspect, accused or witness in respect of his consent, what will be the defence of the investigator; and if the only Independent Witness has re-located to an unknown foreign country or even gone to meet his Maker, Just imagine!! A big problem is on hand. The investigator already has a very 'good' meal to munch. The probability of losing two Independent Witnesses is much lower than just one. We therefore need to factor in "Probabilities" in planning our work as investigators and make ready the necessary antidotes. It is indeed extremely important for every investigator to protect himself very well from any slip or oversight that might create any kind of embarrassment for himself or his Organization. The investigator should never trust any person who appears before him to give a Statement, or take his own safety for granted at any time in his work.

Now, what happens when an Investigator declines to write a Statement for and on behalf of a suspect, accused or witness? In much the same way, we have to permit the accused, suspect or witness to nominate any person of his own choice to do that for him. We will need, as well, to ensure such arrangement is accurately recorded on the Statement Form at the beginning of the Statement.

Then at the end of the Statement we must ensure that we cause the entire Statement to be read over to the accused, suspect or witness in the same language or medium of communication that he understands well. When he acknowledges the content as his true Statement made out of his own very free-will, he is then made to sign or thumb-print immediately below the last full stop of his Statement (as done for every normal Statement), with his full name, date and time the Statement was made clearly indicated just below.

The Case Officer and The Independent Witness will also counter-sign with their respective full names, designation, date and time.

Then, we can make accused, suspect or witness sign or thumb-print against it, not forgetting the date and time. The Independent Witnesses as well as the Investigator will also sign likewise. This means the investigator has indicated that the accused, suspect or witness has accepted the said Statement as his true Statement given out of his own free-will, in principle.

From here, it will equally become necessary for the suspect, accused or witness, as the case may be, to also acknowledge in writing immediately below the above certification, that: *I, Suspect, Accused, Witness ABC certify that the above Statement has been read through to me in XYZ language which I understand and speak very well and that I accept same to be my true Statement given out of my own free-will.*

For instance:

CERTIFICATE {By Investigator}

"I CERTIFY THAT THE ABOVE STATEMENT HAS BEEN READ OVER TO SUSPECT/ACCUSED/WITNESS FERDINAND MANGOES IN XYZ LANGUAGE WHICH HE APPEARS TO UNDERSTAND AND SPEAK VERY WELL, AND ACCEPTS SAME AS HIS TRUE STATEMENT GIVEN OUT OF HIS OWN FREE-WILL."

_____

Sign/Right Thump-Print(RTP)
{Accused/Suspect/Witness}
Date & Time.

_____

Sign: Case Officer
(Rank, Date &Time)

_____

Independent Witness
Full Name, Date&Time.

_____

Independent Witness 2
Full Name, Date & Time.

CERTIFICATE {By Accused, Suspect}

{Accused/Suspect/Witness): I am Ferdinand MANGOES of H/No. 123, Kale City. I certify that the above Statement has been fully read to me in the XYZ language, which I speak and understand very well, in the presence of Independent Witnesses Abinadab Oze' of H/No TY/78D, Kale City, and Obisi Bengon of H/No. MN-39, Lungu, and that I accept the content as my true Statement given out of my own free-will.

The endorsements are just the same as above, except that the positions of the Case Officer and that of the Suspect/Accused/ Witness will swap.

CIRCUMSTANCES UNDER WHICH A STATEMENT MAY BE TAKEN FOR AND ON BEHALF OF AN ACCUSED, A SUSPECT OR WITNESS

Some of the tangible reasons for which the Statement of an accused, suspect or witness may be written for and on his behalf by another person nominated by him are:

1. If the person making the Statement has lost both hands, or the one that he can write with, at the time of making the Statement; or

2. At the time of making the Statement, the person's hand used for writing, is in some kind of visible or proven medical condition that cannot by any means enable him to write his own Statement; or

3. If the person making the Statement does not understand and/ or cannot write the official language to be used in writing the Statement. Here, the presence or services of a very reliable interpreter as well as an Independent Witness who is very conversant with the medium of expression of the accused, suspect or witness shall be paramount. Fancy the accused,

suspect or witness is dumb. We shall need a very reliable person quite conversant with the SIGN LANGUAGE. The Independent Witness will also, preferably, have to be very conversant with that medium of expression of the accused, suspect or witness.

SPECIAL NOTES:

Take special note of the following also:-

(a) The Investigator should avoid nominating himself to write a Statement for and on behalf of an accused, a suspect or witness irrespective of any direct or indirect relationship. A witness can turn a suspect or an accused person; and these can adopt any position, when that becomes necessary to them, at any time, in order to exonerate themselves from the case in which they are involved or suspected of involvement.

(b) Some accused, suspects or witnesses prefer or demand that their Counsels be present before they can make any Statement to the Investigator. Permitting that may not be bad, except that such lawyers will not be allowed to interfere with or influence the procedures required for taking down Statements of suspects, accused, or witnesses as well as with the content of the Statement. The only duty of such Counsels will be to ensure that the rights of their clients (accused, suspects or witnesses) are not violated by the Investigator but that due process is professionally observed.

The Investigator will also ensure he picks no quarrel or unnecessary argument with such Counsels or clients, even in the face of provocation; that could be a strategy. He should treat them politely while remaining resolute and principled on the job. Picking a quarrel with Counsels of suspects, accused or witnesses, no matter the provocation, may collapse the entire objective of an investigation.

(c) Do not dispense Statement Forms to suspects, accused or witnesses or their relations, including influential persons, to take home, to their offices or to other places of privacy to write their Statements at their own convenience. That can either be very dangerous or may not be helpful, eventually.

CHAPTER 7

MODUS OPERANDI

"Modus Operandi" (M.O.) is a term in investigation that literally means "Methods Of Operation". M.O. has to do with the totality or set of factors that are associated with a particular criminal activity or offence. These factors enable one to study or know the **patterns and intent** of specific crimes/offences over a period of time and hence help immensely in the prevention of crimes/offences. Each of the elements or factors of the M.O. is critical in the effective and efficient management and/or prevention of any crime or offence.

Certain Security Systems have not been successful in efficiently and effectively dealing with specific crimes/offences partly due to the lack of painstaking efforts to **study every crime very systematically and then identify and analyse carefully the applicable elements of the M.O.**

Below are the factors/elements of the M.O. :

1. **TIME**

    This refers to the specific moment or period of day, time of week, month, year, decade, etc that specific crimes are committed. Some time ago, armed robberies were for instance carried out mainly in the night and deep on the highways. Of late they are carried out any time and anywhere. This implies a change in the M.O. in respect of *Time*, for the crime of armed robbery, on a general basis.

    Note that "time" here also means the specific *hour* of the day, the specific *day* of the week (Tuesdays, Fridays, etc); the specific period of the **month** (1ˢᵗ week, 2ⁿᵈ week, etc); or the specific month of the **year** (January, May, etc). That is to say certain crimes normally occur in say, January or every 2ⁿᵈ week of the month, or on Tuesdays, or in the early mornings, and so on.

"Time" in this context can also mean *a period of Rule, Government or Administration or season.* For instance, very destructive fire outbreaks have occurred at the main markets within the first two months of every year, for the past five years, in a certain West African country. With this pattern of occurrence, one can certainly smell a rat.

2. PLACE

This refers to the specific *Venue* and/or general environment where an event or crime commonly takes place or took place. That is, the type of places where specific crimes are committed over a period of time. For instance, as we just saw, sometime ago armed robbery took place mainly on the highways and in the bushes. Today they occur everywhere; the perpetrators know no limits this time. In the above example involving fire outbreaks, the fires start nowhere but at the biggest markets in the two biggest cities of that country. That certainly must give cause for concern.

3. MOTIVE

"Motive" refers to the INTENT of a specific crime or offence. It is the main aim or reason why a crime or an offence is/was committed. Let's suppose two men armed with deadly weapons broke into a rich man's house one night. They shot the rich man dead and fled. They did not touch any other thing in the house, not even a single note of the money they found the rich man counting openly at his hall. Here, you can see that the INTENT or MOTIVE of the two armed men was "***just to KILL the rich man***" and not to rob him of his property.

On the contrary, granted that the two armed men in question broke into the said house and stole ONLY CASH, the INTENT of the criminals would be to "steal cash", not just stealing, but to steal cash, because they did not steal any other thing apart from cash - and they needed just cash and nothing else.

Now, in these two simple examples, we notice the criminals had only one intent on each occasion. There are times when criminals would do all sorts of things. It is possible to have more than one intent in a single crime, therefore.

4. **COVER**

This refers to the set of measures adopted by criminals or offenders to **disguise or conceal a criminal operation.** It may be a story (cover story), a physical disguise, masking, etc. In recent times virtually all hard drug pushers, when arrested, claim *"they were only acting as couriers for a fee…"* Perhaps within their circles, that is an "internationally acclaimed" Cover Story. A newspaper recently reported the arrest of four suspected dealers in heroin, a narcotic drug. The story indicated that upon interrogation, the kin pin *claimed the items, contained in two travelling bags, had been given to him in another country by a friend whose name the kin pin only gave as "PUSH" to be delivered to an unknown person in the capital* of the arresting country.

A similar story was also published in another newspaper in the same country of arrest also quite recently, about the busting of a lady at the airport of a far away country. She happened to be a citizen of the above arresting country. Upon interrogation she was reported to have also given a similar cover story.

This gives the indication that in the drug trade world, for the time being, a convenient cover to the cartels is to say *"the consignment was given to me by a friend to be given to another person I had never met"* when intercepted.

5. PAL

Pal refers to the <u>*number of persons*</u> that undertook a particular crime or offence. In the example under "Motive" above, "<u>*two men*</u>" went to kill the rich man. The PAL in this case is therefore "two (2) men".

6. TRADEMARK

This is the profession or specialty of the criminal(s)/offender(s) exhibited in a specific crime or operation. Sometimes when one studies crimes very carefully, one will notice that certain crimes were committed so expertly that ordinary hands can hardly be suspected. That suggests that certainly persons with expertise in a particular profession or occupation must be involved, e.g. a carpenter, welder, technician, steel bender, blacksmith, an accountant, and so on. This is the "*Trademark*" of the criminal(s). Here again, a number of Trademarks could be at play in a single crime.

7. TRANSPORT

This refers to the type of transport used by criminals in an operation. That is, did they come on foot, on bicycles, on motor vehicles, and so on. Here we pay attention to facts like *the Registration Number(s) of the vehicle(s), if any; the colour, make and model; or on bicycles; on foot; by air, peculiar inscriptions/marks, etc.* Let's note here again, that the number of occupants of these vehicles form part of the "PAL" as discussed earlier, provided all of them took part in the crime in question.

8. MEANS

This refers to the type of tools, equipment, chemicals, weapons and/or other items used to commit an offence/crime at a particular time and place. E.g. Grenade, AK-47 Assault Rifle, crow bar, screw driver, Hack-saw, glass-cutting tools, chisel, etc.

9. **METHOD**

   Method has to do with the **order, steps and/or efficient habits** employed by a person or group of persons to commit a crime/offence. In the example cited in item 3 above, did the robbers enter the house by scaling the fence wall at the backside or by a normal entry through the main gate; or did they cut out an opening in the back door; did they give sardine (tinned fish) to the dogs to put them to sleep, etc.

10. **STYLE**

    This is the _DISTINCT_ or _PECULIAR MANNER_ by which a particular crime or offence is/was committed. For instance, assuming the robbers referred to above scaled the fence wall and entered the house: that is their METHOD. But when it comes to HOW they scaled the fence wall, that is the style. Did they use a ladder? Did they go the monkey way where they mounted one another's shoulder? Or how? Did they climb a mango tree just behind the fence wall and took advantage of its branches to launch into the house? Did they leave any trace/mark anywhere or there was absolutely nothing? Etc.

11. **COMMUNICATION** This refers to the medium by which information is exchanged among criminals in the course of an operation. This may be by specially pre-arranged signals, whistling, mobile phones, walkie-talkies, as well as the kind of language spoken by them in a specific operation.

12. **TARGET**

    This refers to the Class of People, Organizations, Places, Installations, Objects, Individuals, etc that **a criminal intent is directed at or aimed at**. E.g. The President, The Chief Justice, The Opposition Political Party Leader, Traditional Leaders, Akosombo Dam, Independence Square, Specific Countries, etc.

Note that *target* is not the same as *motive.* Earlier, under "motive", these two issues were brought to play. The "Motive" of the two armed robbers was to "**kill** the rich man". The main action in the "motive" (i.e. *kill*) is directed at somebody or something - in this case, "the rich man". The *rich man* in that illustration is the TARGET of the main action.

13. **NUMBER** *Number* here refers to *the FREQUENCY* of a particular crime/offence within a specific period of time and in a specific environment or area. That is, the number of times an offence or crime takes place within a particular time and place. For instance, in the year 2002, there were *twenty (20) armed robberies* in just the first week of January in a certain country. **The frequency** of this particular crime within the specific period of time and place is **TWENTY (20) and this is termed "NUMBER" in** *Modus Operandi.* It should not be *confused* with **the Number of people who TOOK PART IN THAT PARTICULAR CRIME**, *otherwise called the PAL.* These are different issues altogether.

14. **GENDER**

This answers the question as to the proportion of males and/or females that took part in a specific crime. Some years back one never heard of a woman or women actively taking part in field operations as armed robbers; today the situation has changed and the women are even more dangerous than the males.

15. **AGE**

This refers to the ages, or age group(s), of the criminals in a particular case or criminal operation at a particular time and place. It is one of the most important elements of the M. O. It draws Governments', or Policy Makers', attention to which section of the society appears deadly and how that can adversely affect State Security and overall National Development. Take for instance a country in which all armed robberies are committed by youthful persons aged between 15 and 27years. This certainly is a very,

very deadly threat not only to the economic development of that country but more dangerously to the security of that State. If for nothing at all, this is about the age group that terrorists might prey on, especially in the wake of unemployment in that country. This is one reason why the M.O. of crimes need to be expunged and expounded.

16. **CLAN** This refers to the tribe, ethnic group or origin of each participant or suspect in a specific crime or offence at a particular time and place. In certain countries, specific crimes are relatively more common among specific ethnic groups. It is better not to cite any examples here, you hopefully agree.

17. **RACE**

By *race* we mean the nationalities of the individuals involved or suspected of involvement in a specific crime at a particular place and time. Nationals of a particular Country, for instance, are very notorious of all manner of criminal behaviour across the globe; notable among such crimes are armed robbery and cyber fraud (commonly called **419** in Ghana). So also are nationals of a certain country as well as persons travelling from a particular Atlantic Ocean country suspected all over the world of being into cocaine.

18. **STATURE**

This gives a description of how each of the criminals is physically built: whether stout, slim, short, tall, etc. A terrorist attack executed by only persons of a specific stature will naturally provide some easy clues for investigation, relative to the area of the offence.

19. **SKIN** "Skin" and "Race" are not the same in this context. 'Skin' here refers to the physical appearance of the 'external body' of each of the criminals *at the time of a particular operation.* Here the race or clan does not matter always. There are a lot of indigenous West Africans with very light skins, for instance; and there are several indigenous Asians also with dark skins.

20. **ROUTE**

This refers to the "direction of approach and exit or escape" of persons in carrying out a specific criminal operation. This is especially important in international and/or organised crimes notably involving arms and ammunition, hard drugs, human trafficking, money laundering, pirating, terrorism, to mention just a few. In relative terms, one can talk of channels/direction of approach/entry and escape/exit of criminals in an operation.

In criminal monetary transactions one can talk of the "Route" as *Western Union Money Transfer and the various other forms of financial transactions.*

21. **APPEARANCE**

Over here we are talking of the costume used by each member of the gang in a specific Criminal Operation, not necessarily as Cover. In the same operation, some of the criminals might be in very ordinary dress with or without masks; others in military tops or down only and some in female dresses and so on, and the emphasis is on '**not necessarily as a Cover**'. Some or all of the gang might be spotting identical bangles on a particular wrist and things like that. Visible physical features on the body of any member of a gang, including the thickness of moustaches, beards, limb deformities are also part of a criminal's appearance. All these petty but very important peculiarities need to be noted of criminals in an operation.

22. **STRENGTHS:**

Where do the criminals draw their strengths from? Who supplies them with Cash, Arms and Ammunition, Vehicles? Who provides safe houses for them? Who sell their booties for them? Who provides legal backing or support? Who aides training? What terms or agreements are attached to all these services? Etc. This is particularly necessary with exercises involving terrorists.

23. **BENEFICIARY/CONSUMER**

Here, we are talking about who enjoys the bootie or receives it. How? When? Where? Note here for a fact that it is common knowledge that certain unsuspecting influential persons organize and fund armed robbery for instance.

IMPORTANCE OF MODUS OPERANDI

The importance of Modus Operandi is immense and include:

(a) For committed crimes where there are no apprehensions, a good study of the M.O. provides very useful clues that help to, for instance, close in on the criminals in contention.

(b) A good study of the M.O. also enables *the pattern and intent* of specific crimes *to be identified* for the purpose of dealing more effectively with such situations in the society.

(c) It helps to effectively monitor and compare, if any, the increasing sophistication of criminals or their activities in a country from time to time and from place to place, and to counter them, if possible.

(d) It enables investigators to determine where criminals might be drawing their strengths from. For instance, supposing terrorists operating in a border area initially used locally manufactured pump-action guns and machetes to carry out their atrocities; then after a short-while they abandoned that and used AK-47 Assault Rifles and have since switched over to the use of mounted heavy military artillery. This trend of affairs immediately should suggest a lot of very sensitive issues, security-wise, to the investigator:

    (i) Organized military and other special training might be going on for the criminals somewhere (either within the country or just outside the borders, not necessarily in their area of operation);

(ii)   The terrorists might be receiving good support (in cash, equipment, trainers, etc) from 'very wealthy sources' - countries, organizations and/or individuals.

(iii)   many more>

(e) M. O. helps in the formulation of policies by Governments, Organizations, etc, to address critical issues that plague societies and ensure peaceful co-existence in the populace, among others.

FACTORS THAT INFLUENCE CHANGES IN THE MODUS OPERANDI OF CRIMINALS

A few of the factors that might influence changes in the Modus Operandi of criminals are:

(1) The degree or level of punishment unleashed on arrested colleagues by the Police, the Law Courts or Ordinary Members of the Public (instant justice);

(2) Strategies of the Police, Military, Intelligence Agencies, etc, used to round up their colleagues or counter their criminal operations. *Mind you, just as Security Officers are busy studying the M.O. of criminals, the latter is at the same time equally busy monitoring the intention of Security Agencies against them, **and that is why we find that criminals, most of the time, appear to be ahead of the Security Agencies in strategizing their operations.*** The criminals mostly act first before Security Agencies begin to study and pursue them. In a few societies, however, Security Agencies are sometimes ahead of the criminals; and even that, it is not so easy, since criminals can hardly be predicted in 'certain situations'.

(3) The type of equipment used by the Security Agencies to counter their criminal operations;

(4) Open threats by Governments and/or members of the public to deal ruthlessly with them (criminals);

(5) Improvement in security systems surrounding respective targets of the criminals;

(6) Own failures in previous criminal operations or attacks;

(7) Studies in films mostly from foreign sources;

(8) Media Reports and bashing.

CHAPTER 8

REPORT WRITING

Report writing is an art. It is just like an artist drawing, say, a human figure. One cannot expect a human figure to stand out with the stomach on top, followed by the feet, then the neck, the thighs, the chest, the legs, the buttocks and the head joined in that order. Can you sketch these together in that order from top (stomach) to bottom (head). What a human figure that will be!

So, just as there are principles in art such that a human figure is seen as a human figure and so on, so it is in Report Writing. ***A Report must paint a DISTINCT or CLEAR PICTURE of an issue or case to the reader.*** It must be clearly understood by all who read it.

We shall begin with the *content* of a typical Report. We need to know what we are going to write in a Report, first and foremost. Facts presented in a Report MUST satisfy the following conditions:

1. *Clarity*

The language and facts presented in a Report must be very clear and hence quite comprehensible.

2. *Conciseness*

Mention the main important facts. Avoid irrelevant information. Go straight to the point.

3. *Precision*

Be exact or accurate in presentation. Say exactly what you want to say. Present concrete facts. Do not confuse the **FACTS** of an investigation with your **opinion** or that of another person. Facts and opinions are not the same. **Facts are PROOFS** obtained in the course of an investigation; **Opinions are an individual's own ASSUMPTION or PRESUMPTION** about the issue(s) in contention. Any mistake here can create serious problems even for the investigator. Unfortunately this is an area where many investigators miss the mark and end up launching innocent poor and helpless people into diverse unpleasant situations such as wrongful convictions and wrongful dismissals. Sometimes that can even mislead governments into wrongful policy formulation, etc. We need, therefore, to be very cautious and avoid such misdeeds.

4. *Orderly Presentation*

All facts should be presented in an orderly manner. The presentation should flow smoothly such that whoever reads your Report would want to read it again; and not just that, but would more especially find the Report flowing naturally to its end.

5. *Objectivity*

This refers to factual fairness and honesty. **No personal feelings, emotions, biases and things like that should be introduced into a Report.** Don't allow anyone to instruct you as to what to put in your Report. Never!! One can pay very dearly for it unexpectedly and there might not be any remedy.

6. *Up To Date*

A Report must be very current. It must contain or include all the current information required.

7. *Timeliness*

Avoid delays in the **writing** and **presentation** of Reports. When Reports are delayed, they can either lose their value or cause unnecessary harm to an individual, Organization or the State. It is therefore not the best to unjustifiably delay investigation Reports: either **slugging** to write the Report or writing it early but **submitting it late** should be avoided always.

8. *Choice Of Words/Expressions*

Avoid the wrong choice of words/expressions. Never use any word or expression anyhow or that you are not quite abreast with, even if you feel you understand it. A single word/expression used in a wrong context can change the whole meaning of your Report and hence mislead decisions on it.

9. *Completeness*

Every Investigation Report must endeavour to answer the basic questions: **What, Who, Where, Which, When, Why, Whom and How.** Avoid presenting half-truths or **unverified information**.

10. *Figures*

Except for dates, always express all figures in words also. Fraudulent behaviour should not be under-estimated anywhere and at any time.

11. *Diagrams/Sketches*

Some investigation Reports require diagrams/sketches for specific clarification. Do well to present very clear and accurate diagrams/sketches, taking note of special reference features/landmarks and cardinality where these are necessary.

12. *Abbreviations*

Avoid this. 'Abbreviations' are not the same as *Acronyms*. All words/names must be written fully.

For instance, "Med. Dir." Should be written as "Medical Director"; and "Veep" should be written "Vice President" and so on. The essence is to make do for precision and clarity.

13. *Acronyms*

In the use of acronyms, the full expressions (or names) should be written first followed by the appropriate acronyms. E.g. Civil Servants Association (CSA), Ghana Medical Association (GMA), and so on. The acronym is subsequently used instead of the full expression throughout the rest of the Report. The essence is to ease reading and also to save time.

14. *Spelling Of Words*

Always check on the correct spelling of all words and names you are not sure of before using them. Note, for instance, that "advice" and "advise" do not carry the same meaning; so also are "stationary" and "stationery". Similarly, "Adzei, Adjei and Agyei" are not the same even though they sound the same. Compare also "Botwe, Botchway and Botchwey". They are not the same. We saw this when looking at Planning in Chapter 2.

The legal consequences of such errors, when committed in Report Writing, can be quite damaging and disappointing.

Structure of a Report

Investigation Reports are presented in various ways depending on the form of investigation conducted. These Reports are generally presented either as Memoranda or "Normal" Reports. Like any other report, a typical investigation report is normally structured along the following lines:

(i) Classification

The handling of Investigation Reports matter very much. They need to be protected from wrong hands. They are therefore classified, subject to their content, to indicate the level of secrecy that their handling should attract. Reports are classified mainly as TOP SECRET, RESTRICTED, SECRET, CONFIDENTIAL or PERSONAL. The investigator must therefore ensure that all his Reports are appropriately classified before submission (See Planning in Chapter 2).

(ii) **Reference Number**

This helps a lot when making subsequent reference to related Reports, and also for the purposes of easing storage and retrievals, among others

(iii) **A Heading/Title**

This refers to a very short wording that throws sufficient light on the subject matter of the investigation. It should just be mild (not sensational) and ***concisely reflective of the true content*** of the Report.

iv) **Date**

The date of a report must be current and accurate. Avoid back-dating reports. In certain Reports, at least two dates appear: One is the "Date Of Report" and the other is the "Date Of Information" and these are mostly used in Intelligence Circles and in Interrogation Reports.

(v) **Introduction**

This usually gives a general idea about what to expect in the main or detailed Report. It contains a brief account of the background of the issue under investigation and where applicable, the "Terms Of Reference" or specific requirements of a particular investigation. In fact, this is where the subject matter of an investigation is highlighted to the reader.

(vi) **Summary Of Findings**

In most modern Investigation Reports, the Introduction is followed immediately by a *Summary Of Findings*. This bears a *precis* of evidence gathered during the investigation. It makes for very quick reading for urgent meetings by superiors.

(vii) **The Main Body Of The Report**

This contains details of findings and available evidence. It is here that the investigator brings up all the evidence at his disposal, with all attachments accurately referenced; it is here that he puts up arguments to explain and prove the above Summary Of Findings based on the available evidence. Appropriate Reference should be made in the Report to all Attachments and/or Exhibits. (These of course should be *very orderly and distinctly labelled.)* All Exhibits, Statements and where applicable, Interrogation Reports, should be attached to the written Investigation Report. They are all key components of the main *Investigation Report.* (See Ch.2).

(viii) **Observation**

Next to the main body of the Report is "***Observation***". This is an analysis of the findings of the investigation and *maturity, circumspection, objectivity, truth and fairness are tested here ON THE PART OF THE INVESTIGATOR OR ORIGINATOR OF THE REPORT.* It must have direct relevance to the content of the main body of the report. Investigation Reports are usually analysed along the lines of Policy (Government or Organizational), Security, Urgency, Law, Economics, Social Development or Politics. A good analysis should bring out any of these very clearly to enhance very informed decisions by government or any other consumer of the Report. Sometimes this can be merged with "Comments".

(ix) **Comments**

This comes next. It is the point where the investigator expresses his personal views or opinion on the findings of an investigation. This is done by drawing intelligent inferences from all the evidence gathered during the investigation.

(x) **Recommendation**

This is where the investigator makes useful suggestions or provide intelligent advice in relation to the findings of an investigation to address the problem investigated. A recommendation must therefore be EXPERT, MATURE, FAIR and OBJECTIVE.

(xi) **The Identity Of The Reporter/Originator**

(Signature, Name & Title, Current Date) of the writer comes at the bottom of the report.

CHAPTER 9

DISTRACTION

In this Chapter we shall look at what is meant by "Distraction" in investigation and how it impacts on interrogation, especially.

Distraction may be defined in various ways. Over here, we are looking at it as "turning away one's focus or attention from a specific line of thought". As someone put it the other day: "Don't derail my thinking", when in fact he meant "don't distract me". It may or may not be consciously induced.

Distraction is likely to show up in every facet of investigation, but it is up to the investigator to ensure that they are either minimized or avoided altogether.

Causes/Sources of Distraction:

These include:

i. Congested Offices (use of);
ii. Persons under investigation
iii. The Investigator
iv. Objects in sight
v. Health
vi. Telephone Calls/Sounds
vii. Dressing
viii. Instability
ix. Condition of the Mind
x. Smell in the environment

xi. Visitors/Call-ups from Superior Officers

xii. Noise: radio; music; television set on; use of loud speakers, church, funeral or other public programmes in the vicinity at the time of the interrogation, etc.

xiii. Having Too Much Work On Hand To Do.

Let us consider these in turns.

The Use of Congested Offices

The use of *Congested Offices* for investigation, especially for interrogation, is not a healthy thing to do. In real professional practice when an interrogation is being conducted any person who is not chosen to take part in that specific exercise should not be present or witness it. The Need To Know (NTK) RULE, has to be observed with all the deserved strictness. An Independent Witness and an Interpreter specially chosen for a particular exercise are part of that very exercise. These are persons carefully invited to play specific roles in an interrogation. Sometimes you can even find ordinary visitors, in a Congested Office, trying to examine an exhibit to the extent of even throwing questions at suspects concerning the exhibit. That is unprofessional and can make the suspect lose confidence in the entire exercise and hence refuse to co-operate with the investigators concerned.

Generally, in *the conduct of Interrogation in Congested Offices*, a number of things happen that potentially disturb investigation, if not jeopardize it altogether.

(a) The other Officers sitting in the Congested Office (as an improvised interrogation room) but who are not part of the exercise could naturally be attracted to the proceedings and could be tempted to also start joining in the questioning unnecessarily. Such attitude can easily *complicate* the entire investigation and hence make the work of the actual handlers of the investigation more difficult.

(b) Some of such intruders could even make provocative and/or embarrassing remarks or observations against suspects.

(c) Others would be judging or condemning suspects, even before the suspects are heard in Court;

(d) The situation becomes more embarrassing when sometimes during an interrogation colleague Officers who share the same office (improvised interrogation room) receive visitors or clients who have private or different official business to transact there at that same time. Such visitors or clients also listen in and get attracted to the exercise. Some would start enquiring right at the "improvised" interrogation room: Ei, what is it about? What has he done? and so on. The likelihood that such visitors would keep their mouths shut over what they had come to see and/or hear over there cannot be guaranteed the least.

(e) There would be noise In the interrogation room, an obvious source of distraction;

(f) There would be frequent "walk-ins and walk-outs", or shall I say "to and fro" movements in the "interrogation room". Both Suspect and Investigator would undoubtedly be distracted, as a result.

(g) Some of these intruders would even be receiving and making phone calls while the interrogation is in progress. We would not even delve into the impact of their general physical appearance (dressing) on the exercise and the security risk they pose to both suspect and the investigator.

One can therefore be very sure that such an atmosphere would, apart from its general distraction and insecurity, clearly create an embarrassment for the person being interrogated, whether he is a suspect or not, as well as the investigator. The person under interrogation could be compelled to refrain from co-operating with the investigations any further and the purpose for the investigation might not be achieved.

All these are obviously not the best for an efficient and effective conduct of interrogation and hence must be discouraged.

Now, where and when an interrogator is **inevitably** faced with such a situation, it may be suggested that he, in planning the exercise, may:

1. Select a time when the office would be free from such interference or distraction, e.g. after normal working hours, for his exercise.

2. Courteously arrange with his colleagues to spare him a little time (a specific period of time during normal working hours on a particular day/date) to conduct an interrogation in the shared office. What the interrogation is about and the persons to be interrogated NEED NOT BE DISCLOSED.

3. Liaise with the Commanding Officer of the Unit, OR, the most senior person at the office, for the purpose of the specific investigation, to set aside one of the rooms, when need be. Where there is a permanent interrogation room at a carefully chosen location too, that is better.

Dressing

When we talk of *dressing* here, we do not just mean *the costume or attire* but the *totality of the appearance* of a person at an interrogation, for instance. The haircut or hairdo, moustache, beard, eyelashes, lipsticks, earrings, for instance, all form part of a person's appearance and can steal one's attention, naturally, and eventually cause distraction. It is not wrong to have any of these. But, for purposes of investigation, *moderation* is preferred. A simple appearance would be helpful.

Dressing has a significant psychological impact on the person being interrogated, as well as the interrogator, being human, and therefore may affect the results of interrogation.

Just as we dress to suit occasions, so do we dress to suit our jobs or specific tasks. That is an essence why even in the Police Service for instance, investigators are not often in the normal Police Uniforms: they wear decent suits, and other mufti, and this makes them appear ordinary, professionally, to suit interrogation or other aspects of investigation that require such touch. The Police Uniform itself is dreaded by quite a number of people and can therefore distract many people.

Supposing you were to interrogate a person in an ordinary assault case and you put on a full Military gear, fancy how the suspect or witness might feel. *{We do not mean it is wrong to carry out interrogation in Military or Police gear, but that it can have an impact on it}.*

Similarly, the person being interrogated (or to be interrogated) can also appear in very "intimidating" costume sometimes *calculated to defeat the purpose of the investigation*. It goes either way.

Fancy a Police Corporal going to interrogate, say, a Brigadier-General in the Army. One can expect a "bully" Brigadier-General to appear in full Military gear which of course, to a large extent, can be very intimidating to the Police Corporal. If one is not principled enough, he might risk being cowed into the 'precincts' of the Military Officer.

Again, a suspect may chose to appear before an investigator dressed in "fetish" gear. The suspect may or may not be a real fetish per se. Here too, many investigators can be intimidated by the "fetish costume" and that can send shivers down the spine of some investigators and effectively distract them. That is, instead of focusing on or thinking out appropriate questions to ask, such investigators so distracted, might rather be mindful of the fear imposed on them by the fetish dressing. Each of them might be pondering what this fetish could do to him, constantly reflecting *"ei, I have to be careful O"*, *"let me weigh my life or my safety against the job carefully"*, *etc.* Things like that could keep bothering the intimidated investigator and obviously get him effectively distracted. This is not applicable to every investigator, anyway.

We need to stress here that **a good investigator needs to be HONEST, FAIR and FIRM on the job.** In this way there can hardly be any fears for any fetish or things like that. Again, yes, there is nothing wrong when an investigator accords the necessary courtesies or respect to whoever that is due, but that should not make the investigator fail or fear to ask questions that he must ask <u>in order to bring out facts that are required of the investigation.</u> THE RIGHT QUESTIONS MUST ALWAYS BE ASKED, BUT VERY COURTEOUSLY.

Health

The health of a suspect or the investigator, especially at the time of an investigation can affect the exercise so much.

For instance, if an investigator has a severe headache or suddenly develops one during an investigation, he is likely to be distracted by the sickness and may lose tract of his line of questioning, or thought, and may also not be receptive of the answers being provided by the suspect at the sitting. A greater part of his attention would be on the sickness.

Furthermore, consider an investigator who coughs continuously. The level of distraction here for everybody in the interrogation room is anyone's guess. In any case, it is important that the investigator makes provision for medical care when planning his work; some First Aid needs to be available at the interrogation room, at least for the use of investigators.

In the case of the suspect, or the one being interrogated, the situation would not be too different, except that any medical attention here can only be administered by a competent Medical Personnel or at a State Certified Medical Facility. Of course, some suspects can feign sickness but still they need to be attended to.

It therefore pays, for this reason, to always have a good vehicle on standby to send suspects under interrogation who might fall sick suddenly to a **RECOGNIZED HEALTH FACILITY** for due attention. But, the bottom line is that all that can cause distraction.

Smell

The next thing we consider is *Smell*. Supposing your interrogation room was cited near a restaurant or a kitchen and during an interrogation the sweet flavour of a sumptuous light soup well laced with goat meat kept blowing into the interrogation room, is it not possible that this can distract both suspect and the interrogator? Hopefully, yes. An offensive odour finding its way into an interrogation room can have a similar effect.

For this reason, one should be very mindful of the need to select a place that is not exposed to such smells, if possible, when planning his work.

Security

Inadequate security at the Interrogation Center can cause distraction. However, this depends very largely on the type of investigation on hand. In interrogation involving high-profile cases like treason, terrorism, arms trade, piracy, murder and hard drugs, one would obviously note that the first thing the interrogators would DEMAND is ADEQUATE SECURITY AT THE INTERROGATION CENTER. If this is not done, and done satisfactorily, the interrogators may naturally not have the full attention on the job. They might be worried about the lack of adequate security at the interrogation center and this in itself is an effective distraction. Their level of concentration on the job, at best, would just be above board. This is because people involved in most of these crimes and their relations cannot be 'predicted'.

On the contrary, an interrogation involving a misdemeanour might not be too demanding for the provision of stern protection at the interrogation.

Telephone Calls/Sounds

Frequent making and/or receiving of telephone calls during an interrogation exercise is another major source of distraction. This is not to say that it is wrong to make or receive telephone calls during interrogation. No!!! The **frequency** as well as the **purpose** are what matter.

In the case of Mobile Phones an ideal thing one can do is to put the phone on 'silence' or 'vibrating alert' so that incoming calls can be attended to after the interrogation. But, for purposes of *vital* or *very urgent* calls during interrogation, the interrogator may from time to time steal a glance at his phone to check if any.

It may however not be too helpful if the person being interrogated is allowed to use his mobile phone during interrogation, especially when he is a suspect. We shall have to use our discretion very much in the case of persons who are not suspects.

Additionally, some kind of arrangement could be made to detail one or two Officers or trusted guards to be in charge of a fixed central telephone facility in the vicinity of the interrogation room who will receive and/or censure all calls so that in case of any danger or other emergencies they can determine the appropriate steps to take.

Objects in the Interrogation Room

Objects in an interrogation room can also cause distraction, *except for specific operational reasons*. These include decorative materials like carvings, drawings, wall hangings, specially designed furniture and souvenirs.

There is nothing wrong making the interrogation room look generally beautiful. That is good. But, that should be done with much circumspection so that it does not distract.

Supposing you entered an interrogation room only to find drawings or pictures of chaotic scenes or drawings/paintings of weapons on the walls, that scenario can affect a good number of people psychologically, thus, distracting them. Certainly, not all persons can be affected by such displays, but a lot of people would feel very uncomfortable for sure.

Furthermore, supposing you went for an interrogation and found a pistol, grenade or AK-47 assault rifle on the desk of the interrogator, how would you feel throughout the interrogation? I trust you could feel threatened or at least somehow uneasy. That would certainly distract many people.

Instability

There are certain people who, for various reasons known to themselves, cannot sit in their seats or at one place for just fifteen to thirty minutes. Such people may not be good materials for investigation. If they are put on interrogation for instance, they will end up walking up and down and in and out of the interrogation room every now and then. This attitude can distract everybody in the interrogation room, irrespective of the level of distraction – distraction is distraction. An interrogator needs to be stable at an interrogation.

Some people too are addicted to smoking and for almost five or so minutes their addiction will force them out to smoke and return a few minutes later to continue with the interrogation. This attitude is not good enough. It distracts everybody. Others drink so much so that they suffer from diuresis. They would visit the washroom almost every fifteen minutes. That can also effectively distract everybody at the sitting.

On the other hand, the suspect or any other person being interrogated may request a few minutes to go out to smoke. The interrogator may allow him. (If the person is in custody or is to be in custody, the necessary security measures must be taken to prevent a possible escape of the person). Such requests could be a cover calculated at something else. If however such request is made frequently, whether by a suspect or not, that will not just distract, but there could be an unfolding agendum.

In any case, the interrogator should not allow himself to be distracted by any of such frequent "interruption", as a professional.

Condition of the Mind

As humans, a lot of things can disturb our minds at any time and at any place. Some are easy to control; others are so difficult to manage, as a matter of fact. Some happen through no fault of ours and others are called for by our own selves in our daily endeavours and attitudes.

We can talk of deaths of very close relations and other misfortunes; unfulfilled missions; serious disappointments; financial pressures, especially staggering indebtedness and routine domestic remittances; family problems; disturbing dreams, legal suits, etc.

When these plague the mind, we can be sure that focusing on an interrogation will not be easy; of course, it depends on each individual. But, on a larger scale, one will not find it easy to focus on the exercise.

Therefore, if the investigator is disturbed in the mind, it is the most serious distraction, as much as investigation is concerned.

Hence, when we must necessarily conduct an investigation and we know our state of mind or general mood is not favourable for the exercise, it will be better for us to honestly opt out because the work cannot be done thoroughly or properly by us. This is better than one seeing himself as **"the best and only man for the job"** and then going in for the exercise only to do a shoddy job, the results of which can destroy someone's future, reputation or create an embarrassment for State Security.

On the part of *a person being interrogated,* distraction may not be as serious as that of the investigator. When a suspect or person being interrogated is distracted, it is the duty of the investigator, who controls the interrogation, to smoothly bring him back on track.

Conduct of the Investigator

It is an undeniable fact that the character, conduct or attitude that an investigator exhibits before suspects, accused or witnesses at any point during an investigation has very much impact on the exercise and even beyond. Some investigators would want to make the persons being investigated by them to know how "big" or "important" they are. They would make unnecessary interjections here and there on what they are capable of doing, the governmental powers they wield and things like that, even without any provocation.

It pays to eschew arrogance and embrace humility and tact. It pays to be hospitable. Frowning and squeezing of the face may not be helpful in investigation.

In the same way, it is not helpful to put up a depressed outlook during an interrogation. That is a demonstration of deflated confidence and can impact negatively on the psyche of suspects, accused or witnesses and distract them and when that happens very vital information might be lost from these persons under investigation.

These do not mean it should be all smiles. Too much of that can send wrong signals to the person being investigated and cause distraction eventually. The investigator only needs to put up a nice but firm face.

<u>SPEECH</u>

Another important aspect of an investigator's conduct is his *speech*. Speech management is very critical in investigation. There are times when one should use formal language; there are times when one would use informal language. These depend on the response of the person under investigation coupled with the strategy of the investigator in a specific situation and at a particular time and place. In all these, the <u>tone</u> and <u>choice of words</u> or <u>manner of presentation</u> need to be censured very much.

If the investigator should use any speech (or words) or any other form of communication that is <u>*detested by a person under interrogation, for instance,*</u> the investigator should do well to note any changes in the person's attitude that might suggest he is already distracted or likely to be distracted; the investigator must immediately check his choice of words. However, supposing you were interrogating someone and that the person proved more co-operative when you (the investigator) used a particular informal language, then all the better - the way is opened for the investigator to tow that path further to draw the person in.

The investigator needs to appreciate the fact that not too many people are comfortable with shouts at them; everyone admires soft speech. We must ask all that we have to ask; we must probe all that we have to probe; we must demand all that we have to demand from suspects, witnesses, etc during investigation; BUT, all that should necessarily be done in a reasonably low and friendly tone, while closely observing the ***facial expression and other gestures*** of the suspect or witness at each question and answer and then making appropriate inferences from that, in case, for instance, the suspect, accused or witness is distracted. *('Interrogation Techniques'* is dealt with in ***"PRINCIPLES OF INTERROGATION" written by this same Author).***

ORDERLINESS

By this we are referring to *how organized* an investigator is in his work. He should always get himself sufficiently ready for every exercise before its commencement. This boils down to "Planning"; otherwise, the investigator risks exposing himself to a lot of distraction in the course of his work. Mistakes or omissions here and there constitute enough distraction.

VISITORS/CALL-UPS BY SUPERIOR OFFICERS

Obviously, it will not be too helpful to keep receiving visitors while engaged in an interrogation or other critical aspects of investigation. The same applies to frequent call ups by Superior Officers to "come and see me", "ask him to see me now", "let him stop whatever he is doing and see me now", and things like that! The investigator may need to ensure that he **adequately informs his Commanding Officer** about an exercise, if such higher authority is not already aware, to avoid unnecessary call-ups. The whole solution to this problem is in fact subjective to the schedules of the investigator to **put the relevant interventions in place** before going in for an investigation.

TOO MUCH WORKLOAD

Sometimes some Superior Officers, would insist on using a particular person for every "special job". Well, there could be justification for that. But, to put it bluntly, it is not the best to always use a particular Investigator for every case that comes up at a particular Duty Station. Too much work load on the Investigator can sufficiently distract him and that will inevitably lower his real work output. That is a solid fact. The Investigator can even break down, physically, and would start reporting sick every now and then. It is ideal to train enough people on the job efficiently and spread assignments to them - at least three to four very competent and reliable Investigators would not be bad for each Duty Station (of course, subject to the population and level of criminal activities in an area).

Overloading an investigator with too many tasks at the same time is one of the most serious means of distracting him, as mentioned above. Overload of work will compel the investigator:-

1. To have a divided attention most of the time;

2. To be always under pressure to submit reports on delayed assignments;

3. Not to have enough time to exhaustively deal with each case on hand;

4. To submit half-baked investigation reports often, even though they might appear to be good ones.

5. To retrogress, with time, both in work output and in health.

NOISE

Here we are specifically referring to the use of television, radio, handsets, loud speakers, etc, in the interrogation room as well as the holding of loud public programmes in the vicinity of the interrogation *at the time of an interrogation.* It is always good to have a serene environment for interrogation.

THE INVESTIGATOR, SUSPECT/WITNESS

All the factors listed or explained above apply to the Investigator, Suspect, Witness or any other person under interrogation.

Control of Distraction

The best way to control distraction in investigation is to **anticipate it in the Planning Stage** and devise appropriate means to avoid it as much as possible. One effective way of going about this is to select a good place and chose a good time for an exercise, granted that the right calibre of investigators are chosen for an exercise.

Effects of Distraction

(a) *On The Interrogator:-*

1. Inability to question appropriately;

2. Inability to make spontaneous critical analyses of answers provided by respondents;

3. Inability to identify useful information given by the respondent;

4. Inability to articulate information provided by suspects, witnesses or other respondents and direct and/or re-direct appropriate follow-up questions to probe deeper.

5. Likely to compromise the objective of the investigation.

(b) *On The Suspect, Witness Or Other Respondents:-*

1. Likely to lose focus and tell stories instead of providing useful information (though sometimes that may be intentional and aimed at achieving an objective);

2. Likely to deny his own answers given at the interrogation (he may say "Oh, No. I don't remember saying anything like that please; go check your records well, please". Etc

These have to be borne in mind in every criminal investigation.

CHAPTER 10

CASE STUDIES

(All discussions under this Chapter are not exhaustive. EXCEPT CASE STUDY 10, ALL NAMES USED ARE IMAGINARY.)

CASE STUDY 1.

Alfred PALMS, Ellen BOOKS and Greggory STYLES are all final year students of Politician Senior Secondary School in a certain Country.

They were due to write their final Examination, organized by the Uest Examinations Council (UEC), the main Examinations Body of that country, in five days time. It was a Sunday and Ellen BOOKS, who was in possession of as many as seven of the Examination Papers in their printed forms sneaked out of the school to share the questions with a friend, Lucy CAINE, in a sister Secondary School in the same locality.

On her return, it occurred to Ellen BOOKS to caution Lucy again to "take good care of the questions. She thus sent a text message via her mobile phone to Lucy right from the taxi she had boarded. The message read: "UEC people are wild these days. Be very careful with the questions. Luv u".

In sending the text message, Ellen, mistakenly, in punching Lucy's number from her memory, directed the message to a wrong destination. The message 'unfortunately' landed on the screen of a University lecturer. Incidentally, this University lecturer, Professor Edward SUGARS, happened to be an examiner with the UEC. So, he took immediate steps to deal with the problem.

Professor SUGARS linked up with the Criminal Investigations Department (CID) Headquarters who also acted very swiftly, using appropriate technology and eventually traced Ellen BOOKS as the owner of the phone used to send that text message.

A search on her by the Police CID, in the presence of her Headmistress, found the entire Examination Papers for Mathematics, English Language, Accounting, Business Management, Social Studies, Chemistry and Physics in her possession.

Preliminary interrogation rolled out the name of Alfred PALMS, a boyfriend of Ellen, as the source of the questions. Alfred had wind of the danger in the atmosphere and was rushing out of his dormitory to hide some of the question papers in his possession but bumped right into the team of Police investigators in the company of the Headmistress and Ellen. Instantly, the Headmistress pointed at Alfred. He was seized by the Police without hesitation.

A search, immediately, on his body found original copies of virtually all the UEC Examination Papers scheduled to be written in the next few days.

Shivers run through Alfred's spine compelling him to mention his colleague Greggory STYLES as his supplier of the question papers and that they wanted to sell them to make some money to pay their school fees.

Styles, however, denied any knowledge of the leaked UEC Examination Papers. A search on him also did not find anything incriminating. He was nevertheless held by the Police CID as a suspect, for further interrogation, having been categorically mentioned as the source of supply of the leaked UEC Examination Papers.

The matter went up for a full-scale investigation after the UEC confirmed that all the Examination Papers retrieved from the students were exactly the same Papers due to be written in the next few days. The entire Examinations were therefore cancelled, pending fresh arrangements by the UEC."

We have been tasked to urgently investigate this issue and make appropriate recommendations *to forestall any future leakage of UEC Examination Papers. How do we go about it?*

To begin with, we ask ourselves: "What exactly is required of us in this investigation?" "What are the Terms Of Reference?" Over here, we are only asked to Investigate and Make Appropriate Recommendations to forestall any leakage of UEC Examination Papers.

Now, the main issue is that "there is an **alleged leakage** of all the UEC Examination Questions meant to be written by Final Year Senior Secondary School Students that particular year". So we shall ask: "**Was there any leakage at all?**" There is indeed a UEC confirmation of the leakage prompting them to cancel the entire examination for that period pending fresh arrangements.

This leaves us to the next line of importance: "**What caused the leakage?**" (NOT "what might have caused the leakage - we are dealing with specifics.) This is the main issue the investigation must seek to unravel. The most important aspect of **the solution to the problem** would not necessarily be the arrest and prosecution of suspects, the cancellation of examination results or the suspension of students from writing UEC Examinations and such likes, but, more importantly **identifying and dealing effectively with the CAUSE of the leakage.** At the end of the day the best solution would be **to EFFICIENTLY AND EFFECTIVELY prevent a recurrence** of the leakage of examination questions at the UEC. If the CAUSE of the leakage is not **well established** and **clearly and sufficiently brought up** in the Investigation Report, we would end up witnessing even more complex dimensions of the problem at the UEC year after year, granted that the appropriate authorities are themselves truly eager to do away with the canker. This is because sometimes investigators would do a decent job but the implementing authorities might, for various reasons (mostly flimsy), shelve the recommendations of Investigation Reports.

Such attitude or practice is very dangerous, if nurtured in high offices of public trust; it is in fact very capable of ruining even national economies and effectively sabotaging national security efforts.

Now, in setting out for the real task, we would need to know **the total path that each Examination Paper travels** - i.e. from the setting of the questions, through the printing, packaging and distribution, right to the examination candidate (1) at the examination centre (2) at the scheduled time and place for each Paper. Then we can deal with WHO handled, or handles, if you like, each of these stages. This will make it easy to identify and hopefully plug the loop-holes in the entire system. It is like a chain: if the chain is not broken anywhere, there will be no leakage; if it is broken then a leakage is inevitable. Very simple.

So, here we go:

"What at all ***caused*** the leakage?" NOT "what ***might have caused*** the leakage?"

We are dealing with specifics, and not speculating, and in this particular instance, we shall as usual, note carefully all the useful information formally available to us.

These would include:

a. The names and identities of the first line of suspects to be questioned - Alfred PALMS, Ellen BOOKS, Lucy CAINE and Greggory STYLES.

b. Professor Edward SUGARS as witness;

c. The specific UEC Examination Papers (subjects) that were leaked as much as these students were concerned (though it could be that they might have sold some off already).

Then, we shall need to know:

(i)   The exact number of UEC question papers that got sneaked out into wrong hands around the time. This may not appear too relevant in view of the fact that the UEC had already cancelled the entire examination, pending a fresh arrangement. But, it would help estimate or determine the magnitude of the leakage which in turn could help narrow down on the line of suspects and witnesses, as the case may be. If say 100 question papers of each subject should be found to have been smuggled out of the premises of the UEC, then we would understand the magnitude of the problem and "who possibly could have access to such big volume of printed question papers and who could carry them out from the UEC premises, and so on".

(ii)   The formal procedures and security arrangements for the efficient and effective handling of UEC Examination Papers and whether these were diligently complied with by all stake holders;

(iii)   Who is/are in charge of the printing of examination questions of the UEC - The interest here is not just in the Printing Press, but more especially the specific individuals who directly print the questions at the Printing Press as well as the schedule Officer or Officers at the UEC.

(iv)   The formal procedures and security arrangements for the printing of UEC Examination Papers and whether these were diligently followed or ensured for these specific question papers whose leakage is under investigation.

(v)   The formal procedures and security arrangements for the packaging and transportation of the question papers from the Printing Press to the Warehouse for storage and whether these were diligently ensured:

(vi)   The formal procedures and security arrangements for the distribution of Question Papers to the various Examination

Centres throughout the country and whether these were diligently ensured:

(vii) How does the UEC ensure that question papers formally dispatched to the respective Examination Centres are not tampered with either before they get to the Centres or at the Centres? Anything can happen under very effective 'collaboration'; a few weak links in a chain of 'stringent supervision' can break down the whole system.

(viii) The true identities of all persons involved in the transportation, storage/ware housing, packaging/distribution to the various examination centres; {see (iii)}.

(ix) The true identities of all persons who have something to do with the general handling of UEC Examination Papers at all Centres - who knows, the questions could have been leaked from a proximal or distant examination centre and not necessarily wholly from the premises of the UEC.

(x) Whether, at the time of the discovery of the leakage, the UEC had sent out any of the examination papers to any Centre and if yes, when was that- (date, time)? to where? which papers? How were the papers sent? by who and received by who?, among others.

{Demand accurate and reliable documentary proofs for all the above}.

From here we proceed to ask ourselves: "Do we use Open Investigation or Secret Investigation (or Both) to access the evidence we need in the most effective and efficient manner?

In this case, we would certainly combine both Secret and Open Investigations since some of the information required would have to be accessed discreetly. For instance, who knows whether the authorities of Politician Senior Secondary School were privy to this leakage of UEC examination questions in order to enhance the school's "academic image". Who knows, also, whether or not some of the UEC Examiners themselves were privy to the leakage of the examination questions, even though the probability here is relatively slimmer because the leaked question papers were many, in the first place, and were already in the printed state, secondly.

Again, we would need secret investigations to establish various information surrounding the printing, storage, packaging and transportation/ distribution of the UEC Examination question papers right to the stage of serving each UEC Examination /Subject Paper to candidates at the Examination Hall.

We now launch into: "How to obtain the required evidence." We shall:

(a) Interrogate all persons whose names show up and who are or could be connected to the production, packaging, storage, transportation and distribution of the Question Papers, right to the Examination Hall.

(b) Conduct Inspection - here we shall need to conduct various inspections from the Press to the Examination Centres where some of the questions might have been officially sent.

(c) Conduct Examination of Documents- we shall need to inspect Invoices/Waybills, etc, on all movements of the question papers right from the printing press to the examination centres. We shall need to find out evidence suggesting any unusual movements of persons (as well as vehicles & other means of transportation), in the respective 'localities' of the examination papers from the moment printing of the question papers started, among others.

(d) We shall also employ elicitation and interviews as means to gather some evidence.

(e) If there are Closed Circuit TV Devices at the UEC, what do they present on their

Screens relevant to the investigation on hand?

We shall then proceed to take Statements from all persons interrogated; whether suspects or witnesses. (Caution, where and when appropriate).

After gathering the necessary evidence and properly labelling exhibits, we shall then prepare our Investigation Report for submission immediately.

It would be very important for us to diligently analyse every piece of information obtained during the investigation, draw very intelligent inferences from that and then present a very good Report, very clearly stating the EXACT CAUSE of the leakage and spicing it with intelligent, practicable, efficient and effective recommendations to prevent any future recurrence of the problem. All that should be drawn from the findings of the investigation.

CASE STUDY 2.

An alleged false alarm was raised in the busy marketplace in the centre of KENTS, the Capital City of an English-Speaking country called BLUEBURNS. The false alarm resulted in widespread looting of shops in the city centre. A lot of people were also injured. No other details were provided. You have been flown from a foreign English speaking country, as a special investigator, to Kents in BLUEBURNS two days after the incident. You are formally informed that the local Police Service were side-lined by the BLUEBURNS Government because of widespread corruption within the Service and consequent mistrust for a credible job.

(a) Suggest how you would tackle the problem.

(a) Bring up some of the major challenges you would anticipate even before being flown to Kents. BLUEBURNS is a country you are visiting for the very first time and you have a maximum of 21 days to complete your work.

For (a), we shall determine:

(i) The Main Requirement of the Investigation (no terms of reference was given).

(ii)   (ii) The Information available;

(iii)   The required but unavailable information;

(iv)   How to obtain the unavailable evidence

(v)   The type of Investigation to use: Open Investigation, Secret Investigation or both.

(vi)   The Operational problems we anticipate and how we can smoothly go round them more especially when the exercise is in a foreign country we are visiting for the first time.

(vii)   Any Operational advantages available before setting off;

(viii)   How to quietly gather the relevant evidence.

These can form the framework for planning.

But, before we proceed to consider these items for any effective planning, we shall have to do some Research, for instance on the Internet, to establish:

1.   The current Political and Economic situation in BLUEBURNS;

2.   The current general Security Situation in BLUEBURNS;

3.   The current specific Security Situation in Kent;

4.   The prevailing seismic and meteorological conditions in BLUEBURNS generally and in Kent specifically.

5.   The general social attitude of the locals in Kent specifically and in BLUEBURNS as a whole. Are they friendly to visitors from across the globe or from specific countries, race, etc? (If you are going to work in a racist or terrorist environment, you can imagine the opposition you would encounter.)

These are vital issues to consider in planning such an operational activity in a foreign country. Such information will be helpful for our personal security, to determine the kind of preparation we have to make and also prepare us psychologically and logistically for the task ahead.

Now, for (a) (I) above, (the Main Requirement), we shall ask ourselves: "What was the ***main event*** that created such a big problem for the government of BLUEBURNS?" It is "*Widespread Looting of Shops*". Then we ask again: "What at all caused or triggered the looting?" It is an *alleged False Alarm*. This alleged False Alarm actually brought about the widespread looting and is thus the most important aspect of the investigation, unless we are given specific terms of reference different from this. Then, in that case, we shall limit ourselves to such Terms Of Reference.

Whatever the case may be, it is the ***EXACT CAUSE*** of the problem that is most important in this investigation. If we tackle any problem whatsoever without dealing with the exact cause, we practically do no work.

For this exercise, we may ask: "Was there any false alarm at all?" If yes, "What was it?" Terrorists charging to seize the city? Lions on the loose?, Apes on rampage? Or what? We need to know. It is possible to establish a completely different cause - not a false alarm, as alleged, after all.

When we arrive at the actual cause of the problem, that will serve as the 'trunk of the tree' from which the main and other 'branches' will emerge.

We now turn to (ii) -" What information is available or unavailable to us?" In this case, we consider the following:

WHAT: Looting of shops; (alleged)
WHERE: Allegedly Busy Marketplace at centre of Kent, capital of BLUEBURNS. There could be other busy places in the city centre for other purposes (not market). (alleged)
WHEN: Time of the day (UNKNOWN)
Date: Day/Month/Year (UNKNOWN)
HOW: False Alarm (alleged)

WHICH: Kind of False Alarm (UNKNOWN)

   Specific Shops looted (UNKNOWN)

WHY: Politically motivated? Terrorist adventure? Or what? (UNKNOWN)

WHO: Who did what? (UNKNOWN). No arrest made.

WHOM: Who suffered what? (UNKNOWN).

From this simple formula, at least we know what basic information we have and what we do not.

Then we come to (iii) "How to obtain the Unknown or Unavailable Information/evidence. Note that even for the basic information provided, we shall still have to confirm every one of them; they will serve as springboards to access other important information.

This is where the main job is. This is where we will decide whether to use Secret Investigation, Open Investigation or a combination of the two.

In this exercise, we shall need much more of Secret Investigation. We shall not have to rush into Open Investigation, even though that will be required. A simple reason is that we are formally told that the local Police Service "were side-lined by the BLUEBURNS Government because of widespread corruption within the Service and consequent mistrust for a credible job". We therefore have no option than to operate quietly or clandestinely for a start.

After we have successfully gathered enough credible information or evidence, we can then liaise with the BLUEBURNS Government through our Superiors (or directly with the BLUEBURNS Government, as the case may be) to strategize for the Open Investigation which will require arrests, searches, interrogation, taking of Statements, and so on which cannot be done without the knowledge of the local Police.

So, we have settled on Secret Investigation for the start. How do we go about it? We shall need to carefully plan this also even before we leave for BLUEBURNS.

We need to plan how to utilize the number of days available to us in relation to the Operational demands of the exercise, factoring in exigencies. For example:

Day 1 - 3: Careful study of the Operational Environment for Good knowledge of the culture of the local people, not mere drumming and dancing or display of artefacts, but their general way of life; good knowledge of the general outlay of Kent and the city centre in particular; good knowledge of the dos and don'ts of the area; good knowledge of the security situation in the country and Kent in particular; spotting; casing; etc. Here a good knowledge of mapping would be required.

Day 4 - 6 :Making of contacts and elicitation. Operational Boarding of public transport - (buses and taxis) to gather information;

Day7-14 :Operational gathering of further information (between Day I and 7, we can also gather some important Information since that is a continuous process).

Day 15-18: Very careful confirmation of the Information gathered so far;

Day 19-21 :Preparation of Reports for submission;

*NOTE: These are just an example of planning our time. At the same time, we shall also need to plan or determine, generally, the possible places where we can obtain useful information in the Operational Environment before we even set off for Kent.

And, for that purpose, we may list:

(a) Hotel Staff

(b) Taxi Drivers

(c) Public Buses

(d) Bus Stops

(e) Sports Centres

(f) Shop Owners & Attendants

(g) Newspapers & Journals

(h) Newspaper Stands

(i) Radio & Television

(j) Bills (Posters), fliers and writings on walls, floor of streets and on other objects

(k) Street Vendors (if available)

(l) The Internet

(m) Community Centres and other Entertainment spots

(n) Clubs, Restaurants and other Food Joints

(o) Markets

(p) Public Functions or gatherings.

Then we come to "what other strategies or principles" in Secret Investigations that we may need to adopt, though some of these may be determined in the course of the exercise in Kent.

A good practical knowledge of Surveillance, including counter checking, shall be very much required. Supposing a taxi driver at Kent identified a suspect who was part of the group that initiated the false alarm resulting in the looting, how can we determine the suspect's "contacts"? Surveillance will be required. We shall be required to have a very good sense of listening, power of observation and, of course, a very retentive memory. These are all aspects of surveillance, as the reader may know very well.

Another important thing we shall need to ensure is the means of communication. Effective and efficient communication cannot be compromised in such an exercise.

By 'Communication' we are not only talking about the Operational Mechanisms to adopt for Surveillance and Base Contacts, but also the language spoken in the Operative Environment. In this exercise, it is English Language and since we are also English speaking, that leaves no extra burden on us. Else, we shall have to "Operationally seek the services of a reliable interpreter or language facilitator" to enhance our work. That notwithstanding, we shall equally need to be familiar with common jargons, and their meanings, used by the general public in Kent.

'Elicitation' is another major means by which we can gather evidence in this exercise. Wherever we happen to be in the operative environment we shall need to be very sharp in the ears. Who knows, someone may unconsciously drop a hint when we do not expect it. We may equally on our own provoke elicitation from the contacts we make, e.g. Hotel staff; taxi drivers; shop owners and attendants of the looted shops especially; fellow passengers on a taxi or other public transport; street vendors, etc.

Other places where we can do elicitation include the Kent market square, restaurants, drinking spots, boutiques, sports stadia, terminals of public transport, bus stops if known, newspaper stands, etc, in Kent.

Besides the fore-going, Radio, Television, the Internet, Bills (posters), Journals are also important sources of information, as seen earlier, that we can exploit in this exercise.

Since this exercise that we are charged with is strategically clandestine, we shall have to protect ourselves as well as the exercise and our clients (the government of BLUEBURNS).

We shall therefore ensure we adopt the best possible COVER at every stage of the exercise in order to conceal the entire operation. We shall for instance have to completely change our appearance virtually every day till we finish this part of the exercise. We may also have to do secret recordings on the contacts that we make. These are but a minute proportion of measures required for clandestine operations.

As mentioned earlier, when we have confirmed all the evidence available to us, we shall then be required to ***submit a Report immediately*** to the appropriate quarters to enable the next line of action to be taken.

The Report should be very well analysed and excellent recommendations brought up to ultimately enhance good decision making for the efficient and effective solution of the problem by the appropriate authorities.

For (b), Some of the major challenges we can anticipate will be:

1. The Culture of the people or public at Kent; i.e. the way things are done there;

2. How hospitable are the people of BLUEBURNS in general and those of Kent in particular;

3. The availability of Utilities such as electricity, potable water, good food and good accommodation;

4. The general security situation in the country of BLUEBURNS and at Kent in particular at the time of the investigation.

5. Availability of good medical facilities and care.

6. Availability of reliable Internet and general telecommunication facilities.

7. Inadequate funding for the exercise. (Use funds very wisely).

Foreign Mission

It will be necessary to register our presence in Kent at our Foreign Mission in that country immediately on arrival BUT never disclose the real purpose of our presence there to anyone whatsoever in the Mission, unless we have specific instructions to make such disclosures.

CASE STUDY 3.

In 1923, a Chieftaincy and land dispute arose between two ethnic groups, the ENSU and the TWABI. The two together occupy about three-quarters of the Central Region of a certain country called OMANBOFO.

Attempts by their colleague chiefs and other eminent individuals from both sides to settle the dispute amicably rather flared tempers with the whole problem degenerating into a fierce gun battle for nearly six months. Several people were killed on both sides, not to mention innocent strangers who lived and worked there.

The matter was eventually settled at OMANBOFO'S Supreme Court, in 1938, with judgement going in favour of the ENSU.

In September, 1948, the tension between these two ethnic groups sprung up following the death of the Paramount Chief of the ENSU Traditional Area. Another round of gun battle ensued resulting in several fatalities.

All efforts to resolve this matter were just wavy; the clashes were "on-and-off". In recent times, they have become more frequent and involve the use of more sophisticated weapons. The latest occurred a few days ago resulting in nerve-racking fatalities including the deaths of some Senior Security Officers and other government officials. Eight persons have been arrested.

The Government, in view of the fact that the clashes were not only a huge drain on its human and financial resources but also a big security problem that needed to be perpetually done away with, has decided to get a firm grip of the situation and consequently referred the recent clash to us for thorough investigation and advice. How do we go about it?

As we saw earlier in this book, every investigation has a specific focus or a specific objective. In the case brought up here, THERE IS THE URGENT NEED TO HALT, A SPECIFIC CHIEFTAINCY DISPUTE for which reason we shall have to establish the "EXACT CAUSE" of the latest clash, most importantly, and relate it to its antecedents. This will enable appropriate recommendations to be made to effectively and efficiently resolve the matter.

In respect of the latest clash, we shall also find out "Who sparked the clash?" and "Why?" In other words, what was the real "INTENT" for re-igniting the conflict, among others.

The critical issues would remain:

i.   The CAUSE of the latest clash;
ii.   Who did what? and
iii. Why? (or the INTENT of the perpetrators).
iv.   What MEANS and METHODS were used by those involved?
v.   Were the alleged combatants locals or a group outside the locality was involved?
vi.   In case of the latter, where did they come from, who hosted them, by what means, and how did they arrive in the area (direction of approach and exit)?
vii. Are they still in the area? If not, where are they? And when did they leave?
viii. Who are their leaders? Etc.

(*See the Chapter On Modus Operandi*).

Additionally, we shall have to establish the background or history behind the clashes. That would help us to make a vivid assessment or analyses of the problem so that proper planning of the task could be made and excellent recommendations made, at the end of investigations, for an efficient and effective solution.

Now, as usual, what steps are we taking to do the investigation? And here we list:

a.   What information is available to us? This usually serves as a springboard to launch onto other portals of evidence.

b. What information is lacking or do we need to find out?

c. What type of investigation are we going to adopt in order to obtain the best possible results?

d. How do we gather the necessary evidence for our report?

For (a), we have:

i. The names of the disputing factions - ENSU and TWABI;

ii. Knowledge that the clashes started as far back as 1923;

iii. Knowledge that there have been several other clashes including a deadly one in 1948

iv. Knowledge of the fact that there was a Supreme Court Ruling on the case as far back as 1938 in favour of the ENSU

v. Knowledge of the arrest of eight (8) persons involved in the latest clash;

We do not know (b):

i. What exactly caused the latest clash;

ii. What are the true and exact identities of each of the suspects

iii. How long did this latest clash last;

iv. What type of weapons were used by the combatants;

v. How many people were killed; how many were wounded;

vi. Who are these wounded people and where are they at the time of the investigation;

vii. What other equipment, including vehicles, were used in the latest clash.

viii. What was the actual motive or "intent" for the latest clash;

ix. When exactly did the clash begin and when did it peak up?;

x. Whether there was any remote cause; if yes, what was it?

xi. Are there any blood, political, academic, professional, economic, ethnic, etc links or undertones to the latest clashes? In respect of background information (antecedents), we shall need to know, among other things:

xii. The exact or true cause of the 1923 clash;

xiii. The exact or true cause of the 1948 clash;

xiv. The exact or true causes of the other earlier clashes, if available;

xv. The details of the Supreme Court Ruling on the 1923 clash (but that should not be allowed to prejudice the findings of the investigation).

xvi. Whether there was any remote cause, e.g. political, ethnic, marital, blood, etc, to each of the past clashes.

xvii. Who were involved in the previous clashes both directly and indirectly;

xviii. Apart from the Supreme Court Ruling, what other measures were taken in each of the previous clashes aimed at resolving the conflict, among others.

Then we come to (c), the type of investigation to employ for this exercise. Here, we may best use a combination of Secret and Open Investigation.

Investigation: Certain vital information may not be easily accessible in a conflict situation like this one. Secret Investigation will thus be of help to us to unearth such vital information or evidence.

Largely, however, Open Investigation would be used. That takes us to (d), how do we obtain the necessary evidence? We shall use, among others:

Interrogation: We shall interrogate all suspects and witnesses and Take Statements from each of them;

Elicitation: Over here, we shall have to provoke conversation, particularly among the public in the conflict zone, to draw out relevant information.

Inspection: We shall conduct "Operative Inspection" of various sites or scenes of the latest clashes to look for Evidence such as used cartridges which can help to determine the type of weapons and ammunition used by the combatants, which in turn can help to establish the possible source of supply of such weapons - whether from government circles, commercial sources, local manufacturers, etc. Other evidence may equally abound at the scene of crime or of the clashes.

<u>*Research:*</u> We shall research into the background of the clashes to enable the Modus Operandi to be determined and appropriate strategies evolved, in relation to the findings of the latest clash, to effectively and efficiently resolve the conflict.

<u>*Search*</u>: We shall have to search the bodies, vehicles, work-places, homes and other known premises of every suspect that comes to the lime-light for pieces of Evidence, but within the limits of existing legislation.

When all these and other relevant steps are taken to gather the necessary evidence, including the writing of Statements by all suspects and witnesses, we then proceed to write our Reports for immediate submission.

Now, touching on the kind of advice or recommendation we can make to the government, we shall only be able to do that after gathering sufficient evidence on the latest clash and thoroughly analysing every detail of every piece of evidence before us in relation to the established circumstances of the previous clashes, including the Supreme Court Ruling. Such Recommendation or Advice to the government should not in any way sound "Judgemental". Rather, it should clearly and indisputably, expound the real cause or causes of the conflict. Emotions and bias of the slightest shade should not under any circumstance be introduced into such recommendation or advice to the government, else ***<u>we may seem to have presented a good report but in effect end up aggravating the problem for the government and everybody.</u>***

CASE STUDY 4.

We are told that*: "Around noon on Monday 17ʰ August, 2009, sporadic gunshots were heard around the Chief's Palace at NOKWARE, a town in the South Western County of a hitherto very peaceful country. The incident happened in broad daylight and in the full glare of the public. The Chief, MOUSTAFA KANKANI, was seriously wounded in the head and had to be rushed for an emergency operation at the Mildds University Hospital in Konko, the Capital City. Three of his elders lost their lives and some innocent passers-by were also hit by stray bullets. No arrests had been made three days after the incident."*

We are tasked to:

1. Conduct thorough investigations into the incident;

2. Identify the exact cause;

3. Establish who were responsible and their intent; and

4. Make appropriate recommendations to check any future occurrence.

To begin with, we must ensure that we **know** and **understand the exact requirements** of the investigation referred to us. We must know and understand what we want before we can plan how to get that.

In this investigation, all we are provided constitute an allegation. It is therefore our duty to confirm or deny each of the issues raised in the allegation, and the main issues are : (a)*Alleged Sporadic Shooting, (b) Three persons allegedly killed (c) Chief Moustafa Kankani of Nokware allegedly wounded in the head and (d) Innocent passers-by allegedly hit by stray bullets.*

Let us consider item (a) for instance. The first question we shall ask ourselves is: Was there any shooting at all on the said date and place, (not even to talk of time yet) in the area indicated? If we ESTABLISH that there was no shooting incident at all in the area around that date, then obviously there will be no need even to think of any CAUSE. But, if we establish that there was actually a shooting incident in the said area on or around the given date, then we would proceed to find out what the actual CAUSE was and probe further.

We can now proceed to ask these questions in response to the given Terms Of Reference.

a. What information is provided in the original request or allegation? That will serve as a spring-board from where the entire investigation will be launched.

b. What information do we need to find out and

c. How do we find out such evidence that is lacking?

These thoughts will bring us to "Planning".

Planning

1. List all the information we have, from the original report or allegations? Match this list with the Terms of Reference and determine:
2. What information we have to look for? Then,
3. How do we obtain this unknown information?
4. Who could be the suspects and what could be their intent?
5. Any witnesses?
6. Who do we interrogate and in what order, if we have to question more than one person, for instance?
7. How do we get all those to be interrogated to respond to our call or co-operate with the investigation: Written invitation, telephone/personal invitation, surveillance to locate and arrest suspects, etc?
8. What language are we going to use for the interrogation? Shall we require an Interpreter? If yes, how do we secure a reliable one soonest? What will be his motivation?
9. How do we obtain Independent Witnesses for interrogation and the Writing of Statements?
10. Shall we Caution suspects or not? (if any is available)
11. How do we access the Crime Scene? How soon can we do that and how do we secure the place in order to preserve evidence?
12. What equipment, Logistics etc shall we need for the efficient execution of the exercise? Are these available? Else, how do we get them?
13. How much funds shall we need for the exercise? (How do we ensure judicious use of same?).
14. Do we have the right calibre and number of personnel to undertake the task efficiently and effectively?
15. Any exhibits available or to look for? How do we preserve them?

16. Various other questions that one can think of, but relevant to the requirements of the investigation. (See Planning in Chapter 2)
17. Report Writing: The content of the Report will depend on the findings or evidence gathered during the investigation. Ensure that all evidence are accurately presented as obtained during the investigation and all attachments also accurately labelled and very clearly and orderly referenced in the report.

For this case, let us consider a few of the items listed above. For (1), the information we have include:

a. The Date of the alleged incident - 17th August, 2009; the time is mentioned but not exactly("around noon", instead of say "Between 11.45am and 12.20pm" etc)
b. Alleged main incident (Sporadic shooting)
c. Place of the alleged incident (Around Chief's Palace, Nokware, South Western County – not specific).
d. The full name and title of the Alleged Wounded Chief (Moustafa Kankani)
e. The nature of the alleged injury caused to this Chief (severe head injury)
f. That the Chief was allegedly rushed for an emergency operation;(is that true?confirm)
g. The location of the Chief (Mildds University Hospital, Konko), allegedly; (but is he really at this hospital or elsewhere?)
h. Three elders of the town were allegedly killed; (what are their true identities?)
i. No arrest made three days after the alleged incident; why?

For (2), "What information we have to look for", we can consider the following:

a. The exact time or period of the incident and the intent for that. Note the alleged wounding of Chief Moustafa Kankani and murder of his three elders. Why, if true?

b. On which date, at what time, by whom and for what reason was Chief Moustafa Kankani sent to the hospital, if he was truly sent to a hospital at all?

c. The full particulars of the Medical Doctor who operated upon him, if that truly took place at all as well as the three alleged murdered elders.

d. The Official Medical Report on him (Not an unofficial one). It must bear the official stamp of the Doctor, indicating his exact status at the Hospital, e.g. Senior Medical Officer, Physician, Houseman, etc.

e. Is the Chief still at the hospital?

f. If discharged, for how long was he there and where is his present location? (for the purpose of interrogation).

g. If the Chief can speak, what is his version of the alleged incident? NOTE: It is advisable, even though not mandatory, to ensure that we obtain a written permission of the Doctor in charge of an in-patient (here, the Chief) before interrogating that sick person at the hospital, if and only if it is absolutely necessary to interrogate him in that very condition. In this case we have to apply our discretion and not to ask too many questions; only the salient ones, just to establish specific evidence on the incident under investigation such as "whether there was really any shooting incident at the said Palace around noon on the day in question. Similarly, if the "seriously sick" person happens to be at home, we first have to seek the permission of a close relation present in the house at the time we want to question that sick person, eg True spouse, offspring, etc and preferably conduct the interrogation in the presence of that same person. In all these, we need to ensure that we have an Independent Witness and also record all communication very well. In case it is not possible to take the person's Statements immediately after the interrogation for genuine reasons, we shall have to adjust to the situation.

h. Where is the alleged injured passer-by? Is he in hospital, at home - where is his exact location so that we can ascertain his exact condition as well as what sent him to the hospital, etc.

i. What is his true identity?

j.   If he is truly injured, any Doctor's Report to ascertain the exact cause and degree of the injury?

k.   If he can speak, what is his side of the incident?

l.   What are the true identities of the three elders who allegedly lost their lives as a result of the 'shooting incident' (The Chief can be of help in this area since they were allegedly in his Palace at the time of the alleged 'shooting incident').

m.   If, so far, there are indications that the shooting incident actually took place at the Chief's Palace, and in broad daylight, who were involved (or suspected of involvement)? Any witnesses too? Etc.

Then we come to the Investigation itself. Here, we first decide on the type of investigation to use - whether Open Investigation, Secret Investigation or Both.

Looking at the nature of this alleged shooting incident, a combination of both Open and Secret Investigation might be more helpful. The Secret Investigation may help to close in on the suspects in the shooting incident and apprehend them. Most of the task will however involve Open Investigation. We shall therefore use:

Interrogation:- who do we question? How do we get them ready for questioning (invitation or arrest)? and in what order, if we have more than one person to question?

Interviews:- this may help in our search for suspects;

Elicitation:- this has to be done, professionally of course, not only in the vicinity of the shooting incident but also at public places where people normally gather or visit e.g. Lorry parks, public bus terminals, bus stops, marketplaces, sports centres, Newspaper stands, etc for information on the incident.

Inspection:- especially of the Crime Scene (and its protection). Is there any evidence suggesting shooting? or any other form of violence / attack?

Documents:- We shall need to assemble all documentary proofs in relation to the case, including the Medical Reports on Chief Oshogbo Karim Musa I, and that of the injured passer-by as well as the Pathologist's Report on the three deceased elders (if and only if they actually died around the specified period). These Documents will be very vital pieces of Evidence for this investigation.

Photographs:- Pictorial evidence in an incident like this is very important especially at the Scene of the Incident. Should any member of the general public have any photographic evidence on the alleged shooting incident, especially Audio Visuals that can be very helpful to us then that will be a material we shall certainly go for?

Others:- Apart from the above, there are several other pieces of evidence that may be needed or that may show up in the course of the investigation.

When all the necessary or available evidence have been gathered, the next thing is Report Writing. This should be done immediately after the investigation. We should ensure to present our findings in a very orderly manner in order to paint a distinct picture of the investigated issue. All attachments, e.g. exhibits, should be very clearly labelled and referenced in our Report.

Findings

For purposes of discussion, we 'assume' that the following findings were made after thorough investigations:

1. The three deceased elders died of food poisoning, instead, at the Palace of Chief Moustafa Kankani *and not by gun-shot wounds.*

2. The Chief was also rushed to the hospital because of food poisoning and not because of any bullet wound. There was no 'visible' wound on his body.

3. The three deceased elders died in the Chief's Palace about an hour before noon on the said date and were sent to the hospital around

noon on that 'fateful day' in an Ambulance. They were all dead on arrival (DOA) at the hospital.

4. There was sporadic shooting, by three armed robbers, in one of the clusters of houses not too far from the Chief's Palace (about 300metres away);

5. The wounded passer-by, a Final-Year Chemistry Student of the local University of Wagon, was however actually hit by a stray bullet as he strolled in front of one of those houses, which had suddenly been clawed in a three-man armed robbery attack, and was rushed to the hospital (the houses were not numbered); he was responding to treatment at the time of the investigation;

6. There was a swift armed robbery attack in a house about 300 metres from the Chief's Palace between 11.50am and 12.05pm on Monday 17th August, 2009. Eye Witnesses testified to that and a further evidence of eleven (11) spent cartridges of an AK-47 Assault Rifle were retrieved by investigators from the scene.

Observation

It is observed from the findings of the investigation that the allegation brought up for investigation were not exactly factual as reported. Different revelations rather came up that are equally of grave concern.

It is suspected that there is a calculated intention to conceal an obvious crime of food poisoning, the purpose for which one cannot just speculate.

Nevertheless, the real essence of investigations has been proven in this case, thus making the exercise worth-while. That is, the true facts have been established.

Recommendation

From the 'facts' of the above investigation it is recommended that the issue of food poisoning, which was the real cause of the deaths in question, be subjected to a full-scale investigation immediately. The need to identify and arrest the orchestrators and also establish the REAL INTENTION behind the crime cannot be over-looked.

NOTE:

From such 'findings' as above we appreciate the importance of investigation and the need for investigators especially, and politicians, people in managerial/leadership positions, the media, the law enforcement Agencies, for instance, ***not to hasten into conclusions or rush information into the public domain; thorough investigations should always be conducted into all issues especially those that bother on State Security, those that can dent the reputation of innocent personalities or that can jeopardize the career of innocent people, and of course, not forgetting those that unjustifiably intrude the privacies of others.***

We notice that the *allegation brought up for investigation* and the *findings* of the investigation are very different. This is the essence of investigation. In investigations, *we report only on* ***exact findings.***

CASE STUDY 5.

A local newspaper said a few days ago that: "The influx of fake and sub-standard pharmaceutical products were on the increase on the market in our country. The report feared the associated dangers in this indiscriminate peddling of all manner of medicines in our country." We are charged to investigate this issue, as a matter of urgency and (a) bring up those responsible for the heinous crime and (b) make appropriate recommendations to address the problem.

How shall we go about it, granted that we do not belong to any health or pharmaceutical Institution or Body?

We begin, as usual, with:

    i.   "What exactly is required of the investigation"?

ii.   What information has been provided formally?

iii.   What information has not been provided or do we need to look for as evidence? and

iv.   How do we do all that?

For this drug case, we are mainly required to establish "Who are responsible for the influx and distribution of fake and sub-standard drugs in our country?" It will be very necessary to specify, also, which drugs are involved here.

The information we are mainly given is:

"There is an alleged influx of fake and sub-standard pharmaceutical products in our country".

<u>*We do not know how true this piece of information is.*</u> So, we need to establish:

1. *Who is the source of the newspaper publication (possibly to provide some leads for the investigation)?*

2. *The specific pharmaceutical products in contention. (Not all the drugs brought in from outside the country are fake or sub-standard).*

3. *How do the drugs come in, if the report is true at all? -By smuggling or through the normal entry points, and from where were they shipped in?*

4. *The particular point or Port of inflow of the drugs.*

5. *Who are involved, or suspected of involvement, in this influx and distribution of the alleged fake and sub-standard drugs in our country and what is their intent?*

6. *What is the existing legislation on the importation of pharmaceutical products into the country?*

We notice that this piece of investigation would be a very extensive one even though it appears to be very simple. We shall require a good knowledge of the current legislation governing the importation, procurement and distribution of drugs in the country. We shall need to seek *very reliable technical assistance* from a good number of recognized professional bodies in the health/pharmaceutical sector such as the Pharmacy Council, the Food and Drugs Board, the Ministry of Health, the National Standards Board, the National Pharmaceutical Society, among others.

We shall also have to do *elicitation* with Border/Port Officials such as The Customs, Excise and Preventive Service (CEPS) and Port Health Authorities.

The media house that carried the bulletin might be the first point of call for us in this investigation. It is more likely to provide us with important leads to the investigation, such as the source of their information (just for a brief), if possible, and other important details such as the exact names and manufacturers (origin) of the alleged fake and sub-standard drugs.

For the type of Investigation to employ in the exercise, we shall use both Open and Secret Investigation, but, of the two, Secret Investigation would be employed more extensively to dig out the required evidence.

Genuine import documents at the entry points can be useful to identify all drugs imported into the country within a reasonable period of time and the identities of the respective importers, among others. Then we may pick the investigation up from there.

Else, we shall have to engage in an extensive and intensive surveillance on all imported drugs on the market. The possibility of the alleged fake and substandard drugs being re-packaged under recognized labels cannot be ruled out.

Now, HOW do we get the required drugs and WHO deals in them, assuming that the media house that carried the news item as well as all the other Agencies listed above were unable to provide any useful leads for the purpose. Secret investigation would be very helpful in this wise.

Then we come to interrogation. This will come in when we are able to apprehend any suspects in the case or when we come by any witnesses. We would have searched their homes, shops, warehouses or stores, vehicles and even their bodies before the interrogation.

Here one may ask: "Why search their bodies too"? Yes, we must search their individual bodies too because it is possible to find, say, an invoice, a sample of sub-standard or fake drug, a leaflet or other pieces of evidence that might provide useful leads for the investigation.

Granted that after all such efforts at obtaining evidence, in this case, did not yield any fruitful results, we do not hastily write-off the possibility of the influx of sub-standard and fake drugs in the country, considering the importance of the investigation. Rather, we may need to conduct extensive surveillance on Pharmaceutical products on the market as well as at the Ports for some reasonable period of time for any leads.

Whether or not we are able to land some arrests, we shall be required to submit a full Report to our superiors on the case. Such a Report should include our actual "findings" and clear suggestions on how to curb the incidence of the influx of sub-standard and fake drugs in the country.

Observation, Recommendation and Comments here would be subject to the findings of the specific investigation.

CASE STUDY 6.

"Francis DIN, a 30-year old driver and caretaker of the Friends Presbyterian Church, Meat Bungallow Branch, is helping the Meat Police in their investigations into the murder of a 12-year old class three pupil of the local Methodist School.

A Police source, who gave the name of the deceased as Matilda Pawpaws, told the National News Agency (NNA) that the deceased was found buried in a shallow grave close to the church premises.

He said the deceased lived with her grandmother at "Horse Park ", a suburb of Meat, where she sold "wakye " for a living. The source said on May 24, this year, the deceased left home to sell "wakye" but never returned. According to the police source, Francis DIN claimed he was cleaning the church premises for the evening service when he spotted a dug-out that looked like a grave behind the church building.

The source said Francis DIN told the police that when he went to inspect the hole he suspected that a human being was buried in it. DIN was said to have reported the incident to the Presbyterian Church District Pastor who also informed the police and DIN was arrested. Meanwhile, the body of the deceased had been conveyed to the police morgue for autopsy". Comment on this case.

To do this, we shall need to answer certain questions in relation to the case. These include WHAT, WHO, WHOM, WHERE, WHEN, HOW, WHY and WHICH.

WHAT happened? A child, Matilda PAWPAWS, aged about 12 years and a primary three pupil of Meat Methodist School has been murdered.

WHO is involved? The actual murderer is not yet known. One Francis DIN, a cleaner at the Bungallow Branch of the Friends Presbyterian Church, Meat, is being held as a suspect by the Police.

WHOM: Who suffered what? *A 12-year old class three pupil, Matilda Pawpaws, is murdered.*

WHY? Here, two issues can be involved: (a) *WHY was Matilda Pawpaws murdered? For what reason?* and (b) *WHY is Francis DIN being held as a suspect? For what reason?* We shall need to distinguish between the two equally important facts and come very clear on each of them. For the start, one cannot pre-empt the INTENT for the former. However, for the latter, Circumstantial Evidence that he, allegedly, first saw the "grave" of the deceased and reported, might be a reason for 'temporarily' holding him as a suspect. In respect of the former it is only a question of the intent of the actual murderer (that is yet to be known after the actual murderer is apprehended and interrogated; an autopsy on the body can also provide useful clues for the intent, especially where and when certain body parts may be missing – that may suggest a ritual murder).

WHERE did the incident take place? We can only *presume* it took place "in or around the Friends Presbyterian Church at Meat" until thorough investigations establish otherwise.

HOW did the trench "discovered" by Francis DIN look like such that when he saw it he had good reason to suspect there was something fishy. Was the trench freshly dug out or what? WHAT exactly attracted DIN to it? These and other similar questions will help to determine DIN's involvement, if at all.

WHEN or on what date and at what time, exactly, did DIN discover the trench in which the deceased was buried? AND *at what time did he disclose his discovery and to whom, initially and subsequently?* Answers to these questions can provide important leads to ease the investigation. For instance, if the day DIN discovered the hole was a Sunday, it is likely there was Church Service in the Chapel in the morning of the same day. Then there could be the possibility that at least a few members of the Congregation might have seen the covered pit too on their way to Church that very Sunday morning, or even earlier. Otherwise, it might look absurd for DIN to have been the only one to have seen the hole in which the deceased school girl was buried since it was located very close to the Church premises.

If the dug-out happened to be an old one, then we may presume DIN might have some knowledge of the murder. He should have seen "changes" in it and reported far earlier than he did since it was just within his vicinity.

We can also ask ourselves: "*HOW* was the murder executed?" Here, there are many possibilities. For instance, the child could have been murdered far away from the area but sent there to be secretly buried or the child could have been murdered in the vicinity of the Church. WHAT could be the exact cause of death? A Pathologist's Report on the Cause of Death will be a very essential lead to establish the exact cause of death.

The above Report could throw more light on whether the child was raped before being murdered in order to cover up the rape; or whether she was murdered for ritual purposes or otherwise.

We also need to know about the background of DIN, especially his criminal records, and something about his associates. We shall also have to do some secret investigation to, for instance, find out about his movements just before the "discovery of the grave", if known, or the murder day (i.e. Sunday, Monday, Tuesday, etc) and just afterwards, if known.

We shall need to establish the specific places or areas the victim normally took her 'wakye' round. Then we would trace the last place she was found or her routine stop points; then from such information we might be able to get some leads into who was last seen with her, etc. In case we found no clues leading to any more arrests, we might need to diligently keep up with Secret Investigation on the issue for some reasonable time to discover more facts.

The possibility of the child being kidnapped and murdered in a far away town and the body smuggled into the area where she was found to secretly bury her there to look as if she was killed in that environment, cannot be ruled out, as mentioned earlier.

At the end of the day we shall need to interrogate all accessible suspects and witnesses. Such findings will form the bedrock of our comments in our Final Report.

CASE STUDY 7

"Police at Chola have grabbed three suspected members of a crossborder armed robbery gang operating in Yolly and Whyna, neighbouring countries, who allegedly robbed a Begotta-based Whynese Businesswoman at gun point a week ago. They are Akin Muller, alias Malu, 20, an unemployed Yollese based in Kiyu, Yolli; Lackeur Buzz, alias Major, 30, also unemployed Yollese based in Quarta-Be, Apukka; and Agara Moss, 37, their Whynese collaborator who is a highly reputed owner of a big Supermarket in Myonne. A search on them found

two locally manufactured guns, an AK-47 assault rifle, (both fully loaded with ammunition), a sharp knife, a crow-bar and five expensive mobile phones.

Mr Quel Aluta, District Police Commander, at Chola, told a press conference that around midnight on February 10, 2010, five armed and masked men broke into the premises of the Whynese businesswoman, Adwoa Doffo, at Chola and made away with several items including four gold wrist watches, nine mobile phones, a ladies bag containing Rhidish and Whynese passports and a large amount of money in foreign currency and seyon that the victim could not specify.

According to Police Superintendent Quel Aluta, Madam Adwoa Doffo, during the attack, identified a scar on the right arm of one of the robbers, Agara Moss, who lived close to the victim at Chola. Madam Doffo reported that to the Police and when a search was conducted at his house, an AK-47 assault rifle and various dangerous materials were found in his possession, thus leading to his arrest. Subsequently, two of his accomplices, Akin Muller and Lackeur Buzz, who were then in Yolli, were lured into Whyna and also arrested. Police investigations said two of the suspects, on the run, had moved to Myonne before the arrests of their colleagues."

Briefly comment on this report.

To do this, we shall need to bring out the "pros and cons" of the report. What is good about it and what is not good, in our opinion.

1. Frankly, we need to commend the Police at Chola for successfully luring two of the robbers from Yolli into Whyna leading to their arrest. That is very good.

2. We shall need also to commend the victim, Madam Adwoa Doffo for being so observant in her environment, an attitude or a quality that led to the arrest of the robbers. That was certainly a major role leading to the arrest of the robbers. This should be emulated by all.

3. "A search on them found…" Where exactly were these items found? In their homes, their hide-outs, on their bodies, on the vehicles

they might be using, or where? What specifically was found on each of them?

4. Does the woman have any acquaintance with Agara Moss such as to know specific features on his body, in spite of merely living in the same environment? If yes, then Madam Doffo should be able to tell one or two of Agara Moss' close friends or associates, who if searched early enough, could yield some useful results.

5. ". . . two of the suspects on the run had moved to Myonne before the arrest of their colleagues." The Police should be commended for acting maturely by not rushing the identities of these escapee robbers into the news. That indicates that the Police are confident in closing in on them without much public support and hence no need to put their particulars into the public domain, at least for the moment.

6. But, why were the Police able to lure two of the suspects from Yolli into Whyna leading to their arrest but did not do same to the Myonne escapees?

CASE STUDY 8.

Armed robbers numbering four in the early hours of Saturday 11th September, 2008, attacked and killed the Managing Director of Yalley Wood Processing Company Ltd at his residence in Brackks Village, a suburb of Cape Five Points in a certain country.

Briefing newsmen at Cape Five Points, Sir Groovy, Regional Police Commander, said at about 02.20 hours on that fateful deep of the night, four armed robbers scaled the wall of the deceased's residence and tied the hands of the watchman, one Ali Baba.

They then used concrete blocks to force open the main door to the house. Sir Groovy said they went to the door of one of the rooms which was then occupied by a visitor who had come to place orders for some processed wood and started banging at it.

The man refused to open the door and so they shot through it, compelling him to open it. He said they collected six hundred thousand USD, a mobile phone and digital camera from him after which they moved to the apartment of Mr. Yalley.

Mr. Yalley had then moved to the washroom when he heard the robbers attacking his guest. They located him in his washroom and shot him twice in the chest without any question or resistance from Mr. Yalley. Sir Groovy said they ransacked Mr. Yalley's apartment, took away a bag containing an unspecified amount of money which was to be used in paying some chiefs the following day, a television set, a video deck and other valuable items, packed them into his (Mr Yalley's) car and sped off.

Sir Groovy added that when the Police were informed they rushed to the scene and took Mr. Yalley to the Regional Hospital but was pronounced dead on arrival. Sir Groovy said no arrest had been made yet and called on the general public to come out with any information that could lead to the arrest of the armed robbers."

Granted we were asked to investigate this robbery case, list some of the important questions we might have to ask. Give your general comments on an investigation like this, bringing out the likely objective of the robbers and what could be the most likely cause of the attack. What is the Modus Operandi of the robbers?

Inquisition

1. Apart from the guest, who else was/were in the house at the time of the incident?

2. Who are responsible for the preparation of cheques and withdrawal of monies from the Bank for the Company?

3. Who else had knowledge about the intended purpose for the money - payment of the Chiefs?

4. Who is the deceased's personal driver?

5. Who drove the deceased that whole day; especially, who drove him home that evening?

6. What was the lifestyle of the watchman, his wife and children, before and after the incident? Any significant changes? If yes, what are the answers to that?

7. How did the Police know that the money in the bag that the robbers took away was meant to pay Chiefs the next morning? Who gave them that information? Could the person be a suspect?

8. What calls were made, received, and missed by the deceased's driver, watchman and Bank clerks just before and after the money was cashed?

9. What calls were received and/or missed by the deceased on the day before the attack, on the day of the attack as well as after the attack (in spite of the victim's demise)? Also, what text messages, e-mails and other forms of messages were received within the same period. Furthermore, was any person sent to the deceased a few days before the incident? Lastly, was there any threat of any kind from any quarters, prior to the attack, directed at the deceased?

10. Did the robbers go straight to the washroom to shoot Mr. Yalley? If yes, how did they know he was right in the washroom at that moment and not in his bedroom? Or, did they go first straight to his room and when they did not find him, decided to search all other rooms in the house, including the washroom? If so, then how did they know Mr. Yalley's bedroom straightaway?

11. If the robbers went to Mr. Yalley's room and did not find him, they would normally detail one or two of their colleagues to search the room for their booty while the others watched around. Did anyone observe any such thing?

12. Did the guest know the money in Mr. Yalley's bag was in the house and also that it was meant for the payment of some chiefs the following morning?

13. Was that day the first time that that guest was spending the night in the deceased's house? If No, since when and how many times has he spent the night there? Who visited him or with him on each occasion?

14. Did the deceased, prior to that fateful day, have any serious problem (quarrel, etc) with anyone e.g. business partner, customer, friend, family member, etc?

15. What is the layout of the house like? What is the nature of access to the house? How did the criminals open the main gate to allow passage of the deceased's car? Any idea about the direction of approach and escape?

16. Did the guest have any mobile phone on him before the incident? If yes, where is it? Which were the calls made, missed and received for that whole day, especially in the evening and late night? Also, why did the robbers not take it away from him? Which messages were also went and/or received by the guest? And when?

17. Were there other people in the house apart from the watchman, the guest and Mr. Yalley at the time of the robbery? If yes, were they also robbed or attacked? If not, why? If yes, what were they robbed of? Were those the only valuable items on them at the time of the attack?

18. Who were in the house hours before the attack?

General Comments

We might need to take some immediate steps, granted the Police had not been informed already? That might include:

1. Inform Police very urgently of the incident;

2. Check from the vicinity - how did the criminals move in? On foot, in cars, on bikes, taxis/other vehicle (any peculiar inscription or visible marks, what make, colour, registration number and other peculiarities)? How many people came? How did they deploy themselves for the operation? etc (See Modus Operandi).

3. The guest said they took some amount of money together with some other valuable items, from him. What is the truth in this? What items? Why did the robbers not kill him instead?

4. In this exercise, apart from cordoning off the scene of the crime to preserve evidence, it would also be necessary for us to take certain urgent measures to capture vital evidence. These include:

    a. Sending quick radio messages round all Stations to look out for the stolen vehicle and the other items that could be sold in the open market.
    b. Look out for suspicious new characters in the communities and report to the Police for handsome rewards;
    c. Police barriers in the catchment area to search all vehicles, including bikes, moving out of the crime area.
    d. Video Recording, checks for Bills or other writings that might be related to the crime, lifting of traces, photography as well as taking custody of all pieces of evidence at the scene of crime, for instance.
    e. Can you suggest any others?

General Comments: The Operation looked more of a planned one than a mere spontaneous attack. The most critical aspect of it is the fact that _"They entered the washroom and shot him twice in the chest",_ referring to Mr. Yalley.

Considering the facts that (a) the robbers did not kill the watchman; (b) they did not kill the guest when they forced his door open BUT (c) on spotting Mr. Yalley they shot him twice in the chest without any question or resistance from Mr. Yalley, and thereafter ransacked his apartment. That suggests he was the main target of the robbers. Then the question is:

Why should Mr. Yalley be the main target? Had he stepped on anyone's toes? Was it that Mr. Yalley was not treating his employees well? Or, was he just trailed from the Bank after withdrawing the cash? Can we suspect the involvement of some officials of that Bank? etc.

The facts available suggest the real intention of the robbers was to eliminate Mr. Yalley; but perhaps somewhere along the line they decided not to leave the scene empty handed, having seen "big cash" for the grabs.

On the other hand, the money in the house could be the target but the criminals killed Mr. Yalley because they knew that Mr. Yalley knew some or all of them - some could be his employees or friends of the watchman who often visited Yalley's house and could mention them to the Police for arrest if he was spared... who knows?

We might also combine the two likely intents and say the motive of the robbers was to kill Mr. Yalley and rob him of his money. That is a possibility.

One of these three possibilities of the motive of the robbers would be brought out very clearly if actual investigations should be conducted into the incident.

Modus Operandi: The Modus Operandi of a criminal activity can properly be determined after thorough investigations have been completed into it. Granted that in the case involving Mr. Yalley's murder such investigation is completed, then the Modus Operandi of the criminals can easily be determined by listing all the Elements of the Modus Operandi and then using the evidence obtained in the investigation to complete each one of them.

For this exercise, below is the M.O. (based on the content only):

A good assessment of the Modus Operandi would help in formulating effective and efficient preventive measures.

For the Modus Operandi of the criminals, we have the following:

1. PAL: Four (4)

2. TIME: About 02.20 hours, Saturday, 11th September, 2008.

3. MOTIVE: To kill and steal money and car of Mr. Yalley.

4. PLACE: Yalley's House, Yellow Village, Cape Five Points.

5. METHOD: Scaled wall into Yalley's house, used concrete blocks to force main gate opened before actual operation and escaped on Yalley's car.

6. STYLE: 1.First, secured route of escape before actual operation; 2. Fired through visitor's door to compel him to open it and possibly to scare the environment; 3. Chose to attack the visitor before heading to Mr. Yalley, the main target.

7. MEANS: Firearms and concrete blocks (bricks).

8. TRANSPORT: Unknown. Escaped on Yalley's car. *{It is not exactly known how the robbers assembled around Yalley's house for the ultimate operation}.*

9. TRADEMARK: Unknown.

10. NUMBER: One (1). {The first time such incident has taken place or come to security notice in respect of Yalley; only that incident is known to have occurred in the vicinity in recent times, presumably, from the circumstances.

11. COVER: No information available.

12. TARGET: Mr.Yalley.

13. COMMUNICTION: No information.

14. GENDER: No information.

15. AGE: No information.

16. CLAN: No information.

17. RACE: No information.

18. STATURE: No information.

19. SKIN: No information.

20. ROUTE: We only know that they scaled the wall into Yalley's house, cardinality unknown, and escaped through the main gate they had forced open.

21. APPEARANCE: No information.

Most of the "No Information" elements above could be answered during interrogation, if not all.

CASE STUDY 9.

At about 07.15 hours on Friday, January 1, 2001, a local radio announced a bloody clash, unabated at the time of the announcement, between two rival ethnic groups at a town called CARMEL in a certain country. These were the AMPESI and BAYIRE ethnic groups. An unspecified large number of people from both sides were reported killed while many others were also said to be critically wounded. The District Police Station, located at CARMEL was also reported to be ablaze. Dwellers were said to be fleeing the area in large numbers. The Head of the National Intelligence Agency (NIA), according to the radio announcement, had been seized by one of the factions and taken to an unknown destination. All roads leading to the town were reportedly blocked and the fighting was rapidly spreading like bushfire in the surrounding villages. The inferno was reported to have started just in front of the Sucker Commercial Bank (BCB) in the heart of the town. The radio station was calling for urgent assistance from all quarters, especially reinforcement of Security details to stop the fighting from spreading any farther.

We are given this case, a day after the fighting ceased, to investigate and make appropriate recommendations to enable the government take the necessary action to ensure permanent peace in the area. What shall we do?

As usual, for all investigations, we start from "What is required of the investigation" or the Terms of Reference and then we plan from there. In this case we are just asked to "Investigate and make appropriate recommendations..." It becomes our responsibility therefore to determine what is at the centre of the conflict that needs to be dealt with in order to curtail all other infractions.

Though a lot of people have been killed and many others critically wounded in the bloody clash reported between the AMPESI and the BAYIRE, the centre of the whole problem that this investigation should focus on remains: **What CAUSED or sparked the clash?** This is what we must establish clearly above everything else.

We are required to make appropriate recommendations aimed at preventing any similar clash in future. This can only be done by DEALING EFFECTIVELY WITH THE TRUE CAUSE OF THE PROBLEM. Arresting the people involved and jailing them as a means of solving the problem is good but that is just a half-baked solution, if not cosmetic. More deadly combatants can emerge with time.

Therefore, the focus of this investigation would be:

"WHAT caused the clash?" In trying to establish this fact we shall also find out:

WHERE exactly the clash started;

WHEN it started (what time of the day, on what date or occasion e.g. market day, political rally day, etc);

HOW did the whole clash begin and progress;

WHO said what and WHO did what;

WHOM - who suffered what; and

WHY?"

We shall also need to know about the background of the problem to help us not only in planning our work well but also in making informed analyses of the findings of this investigation for the purpose of bringing up **EFFICIENT and EFFECTIVE RECOMMENDATIONS** for the solution of the problem. A good background information will for instance deal with issues like "what has been the level of co-existence between the two factions?", "Any previous clashes?" What was the cause of each of them?" When did these previous clashes take place, how, why and where?" "What were the results of investigations on those clashes?

We will notice that the FREQUENCY with which similar clashes occurred in the past, say every three months, on market days or a week before the annual festival, etc, will provide important spices for our investigation. The same applies to who did what? and how, where, and why the clash got sparked off.

It should be noted that the findings of previous investigations on the issue should not under any circumstance be allowed to prejudice the current investigation. The background may be necessary in the analyses of the findings of the current issue and thus assist in making a very balanced and objective recommendation.

With these and similar inquisition at the back of our minds, we can then set out to plan the investigation as usual. We may proceed this way:

a.   What information are we given?

b.   What information is missing?

c.   How do we obtain the required missing information (evidence)?

d.   What is the background? Has the case passed the paws of the law? If yes, how many times and on each occasion who survived? Any documentary evidence, where necessary?

For (a) above, we have:

i.   What incident took place - (bloody clash between AMPESI and BAYIRE ethnic groups);

ii.   Any casualties? - Yes! Many killed and others critically wounded, others rendered refugees elsewhere;

iii.   The town/place where the clash took place.

iv.   The exact spot/scene where the clash started or was concentrated. (Sucker Commercial Bank. CARMEL Branch). This is very important. It will help us to determine "who was doing what, and why, at the time of the incident?" It will throw some light on the justification of each of the persons found to be involved in starting or taking part in the conflict at the place at that time.

v.   The specific ethnic groups involved in the bloody clash(1. AMPESI; 2.BAYIRE)

vi.   Other damage caused (CARMEL District Police Station burnt down).

vii.   Other casualties apart from the dead, the wounded and the displaced: Local Head of the National Intelligence Agency seized by one faction and taken to an unknown destination.

viii. Fighting spilling over to the surrounding villages;

ix.   All roads leading to CARMEL blocked.

Then for (b), the unknown information, we shall need to know, among other things:

i.   The true identities of the individuals who started the whole clash;

ii.   Why the clash occurred. Was there any provocation from any of the factions? If yes, what was it? Insult, teasing, or what?

iii.   Source of Information

iv.   The exact time and date the clash started and how long it lasted. We are only told that "at about 07.15 hours on January 1, 2001, when the local radio announced the clash", the inferno was still on. That does not mean the fight started at that time. We should not be tempted to say so.

v. The exact number and true identities of persons killed on either side; which of them do not belong to any of these factions? Which of them are security personnel/government officials and their relations who unfortunately lost their lives? Of the dead, how many were males, females, and children.

vi. The exact number and identities of persons wounded and their respective locations (hospitals, etc). Obtain statistics as in (v) above and their respective response to treatment.

vii. What is the history of the town? Who were the first settlers? Any antecedents? What were the remote and direct/immediate causes of previous and the latest clashes?

viii. What type of weapons or implements were used by the combatants?

ix. Which individuals were found taking part or are suspected to have taken part in any of the previous clashes and the latest? What role(s) did each of these suspects play in the 'respective' clashes?

x. Who was found holding which weapon?

xi. Who blocked the access roads to the town of CARMEL? When, How and Why? What objects were used to block the access roads?

xii. What is the extent of damage to life and property in the conflict area?

xiii. When was the CARMEL District Police Station burnt down? Who did that? How and Why was that done? Was that the first time? What was the motive of the attackers?

xiv. What could be the likely "**intent**" for burning down this Police Station?

xv. Was it a mere coincidence? Was it accidental? Or was it a deliberate adventure on the spur of the clash? Or was it a planned enterprise?

xvi. Is it true that the NIA Head at CARMEL has been kidnapped? (or any of his staff?). If yes, Who did that? When? How? and Why was that done? Any idea about his location? Any demands by the kidnappers? etc.

xvii. Were there any EXPERT HANDS among the combatants?

Then comes the big question: How do we obtain the required "missing links?" We are at this stage already conversant with how to obtain evidence and shall therefore, for this case, adopt:

(i) <u>Interrogation</u>: We shall interrogate all suspects, eyewitnesses (plus other witnesses) and the surviving victims as well. The leadership and opinion leaders on both sides of the conflict are potential suspects or witnesses.

(ii) <u>Interviews</u>: We shall interview the radio presenter who put the news on air for any possible leads that may aid the investigation, though this may not be critically necessary. We shall interview other persons of interest to us as well.

(iii) <u>Elicitation</u>: We shall have to be listening carefully around the conflict area, and even beyond, for leads to sensitive information. Sometimes we might provoke conversations ourselves just to draw people in. These would be done over a reasonable period of time.

(iv) <u>Inspection</u>: General scene of the clash and specific spot/area where the fighting was concentrated.

(v) <u>Documents</u>: Judgements from the Law Courts, if any; Pathologist's Report for each of the deceased; Medical Report for each of the wounded; any other document that bears admissible evidence.

(vi) <u>Research</u>: We shall research into the background of the two ethnic groups as well as the traditions or customs of the area and see if there is any linkage between these and the actual cause of the clash under investigation.

(vii) <u>Search</u>: We shall have to search the premises (including vehicles, offices, homes) of all persons who are suspected of involvement in the clash as soon as they come to security notice.

(viii) <u>Surveillance</u>: We shall need to discreetly observe the movements of characters in the conflict area over a reasonable period of time for any possible leads;

(ix) <u>Bills</u>: We shall also have to look out for bills or posters, as well as writings and cartoons on walls etc. These could provide us with very important leads as well.

(x)   <u>Photography</u>: There will be the need for us to do photographic recording of pieces of evidence wherever they are found. This will include audio visuals. All these may be done either secretly or openly, as may be operationally feasible.

We shall not forget that before delving into the above means of obtaining information, we have to ensure we cordon off (a) the District Police Station (b) The Sucker Commercial Bank and possibly block all access roads to the town, subjecting persons and vehicles leaving and entering the town to decent but thorough search of their respective bodies and vehicles on which they might be travelling for any possible evidence in relation to the clash.

That is not all. We also have to determine the type of investigation to adopt; whether Secret Investigation or Open Investigation or both. By the nature of this conflict, we shall need to combine both types. Secret investigation will be more helpful in trying to identify and apprehend combatants as well as other persons who might have fuelled the clash. Information will have to be gathered clandestinely, mostly.

After all the necessary evidence has been gathered and appropriate Statements obtained from suspects and witnesses, we shall then proceed to write a comprehensive Report for immediate submission.

Now, in an ethnic issue like this, we shall need to critically assess or analyse its antecedents in relation to the latest incident and bring up the main cause or underlying factor that needs to be addressed by the government or other relevant Agencies in order to ensure effective solution to the problem and very "reliable peace", and not an "uneasy calm" as we often hear, in certain circumstances.

Where and when a **<u>hard and unbiased decision must be taken</u>** against a particular faction or individual for truly being the very cause of the conflicts in the area, such recommendation must be **<u>clearly made</u>** and **<u>soundly justified</u>** to the government or other Agencies charged with ensuring the peace of the area.

CASE STUDY 10.

Somewhere in 1976, there was a violent revolt by students of Whyna Secondary School (WHYNASS), AFIDWASE, allegedly against the Headmaster, Rev. Robert MOUNT. At about 1 a.m., a very loud noise rippled through the dormitories, forcing every student awake from his or her sleep (and even the Masters who lived nearby too). Everybody was running for his or her dear life. Electricity supply had been cut and the entire school was in total darkness. It was a cool Monday dawn; and a powerful Sunday evening Church Service ending just a few hours earlier, could not even put the fear of God into the ring leaders to abandon that agenda. Many students fled for their lives, some naked, others half naked including females, through the dark bushes to the nearby communities namely Osono, Osiem, the Manso New Zongo and the centre of the town itself - in fact, as far as one's legs could carry him or her for safety. Most did not know 'what was going on'.

Extensive damage was caused to school property especially the Headmaster's car and Bungalow as well as the school's "Boneshaker" (Bedford truck).

The Police were rushed in to save the situation that Monday dawn. It was about 0 1.15am when the incident peaked up and one needed to feel the charged atmosphere. The Police randomly rounded up seventeen students mainly in the third and fifth years. They included Edward Puss, Constance Abbrey, Akua Jassie Gladys, Hope Agyei; Fred Ankle (a.k.a. IPB) and Copper Cabana. They were all set free eventually since staff of the school testified to their established good conduct. Apparently, these students were close friends and had gathered behind one of the classrooms not too close to the dormitories, in their dismay, when the Police rounded them up. The name of one "KING K", a third year student, however made the rounds as being the architect of the "alluta". He was subsequently picked up by the Police and detained.

It took a hell of efforts by the school authorities to get students who had sought refuge in town to trickle cautiously back to the school. The school was closed down indefinitely early the following morning and all students ordered to vacate the premises not later than 10.00am that same day.

205

Supposing we were asked to investigate this case and bring up (a) the organizers (b) the cause of the incident and (c) appropriate recommendations to forestall any future occurrence, how might we have gone about it?

To begin with, we might have agreed that that was an urgent assignment that would enable the Education Authorities take prompt action so that the students returned to school quickly for normal academic work to continue.

Given the Terms Of Reference (TOR), we would mainly have looked for the CAUSE of the revolt and WHO WERE THE SUSPECTS, WHAT WAS THE "STUDENTS'" INTENT, WHO WAS/WERE THEIR TARGETS and WHY, at least, before considering any RECOMMENDATIONS.

In other words, what might we have been investigating? We would have been very much focused on "What actually caused the students' revolt?" That would have been at the centre of the whole investigation. Should we have known the cause, then, we could have suggested appropriate steps to forestall any similar situation in future.

We would therefore have asked:

"What information are we provided with on the revolt?' "What would we have looked for?' and "How best might we have accessed such information or required evidence?'

From the report, we *are* given:

(i)   The names of some students randomly rounded up and provisionally held as "suspects": (Edward Puss, Constance Abbrey, Akua Jassie Gladys, Hope Agyei, Fred Ankle and Copper Cabana).

(ii)   King K, is mentioned as a Primary suspect or ringleader.

(iii)   The time of the incident ("about" 01.15 hours on 12th November, 1976);

(iv)   The main target is indicated as Rev. Robert Mount, the Headmaster;

(v)   Damage caused to property (the Headmaster's Bungalow and car, School Truck, electricity supply system)

We would have needed to know:

(i)   What caused the revolt?

(ii)   Was it planned or a spontaneous action?

(iii) Who actually were behind it?

(iv)   Who actually took part?

(v)   What was their intent? Among others.

Now concerning the type of investigation to employ, we would have used a combination of Secret and Open Investigations. Some pieces of information or evidence would not have been too easy to obtain directly from witnesses; secret investigation could have helped matters.

Generally, we would have accessed the required evidence or information by means of Interrogation, Interviews, Inspection of scene of crime, Elicitation, Research; we might also have needed to provide an easy way for people to volunteer information without necessarily appearing before investigators.

We would have needed to cordon off the entire school premises under guard and particularly the Headmaster's Bungalow in order to preserve evidence as well as protect the Headmaster and the entire school from any further attacks. But, one would ask: "why not the Headmaster's Bungalow alone?" The reasons are simply that:

a.   The insurrection took place "on the school compound" but not limited to the Headmaster s bungalow;

b.   There could be vital evidence hidden on any part of the school compound;

c.   In the process of the perpetrators fleeing the school compound to escape Police arrest, very vital pieces of evidence could drop anywhere on the school compound and in the circumstances a very swift action would have had to be taken to inspect the entire school compound including the classrooms, dormitories, the Assembly Hall etc. Should we have come by anything incriminating or suspicious of criminal intent, then that could have opened another positive door for the investigation.

KING K, a Form Three student, was widely rumoured as being the ring-leader. He would have been among the first line of persons to be suspected of the crime for interrogation.

Others to be interrogated would have included the Headmaster, Rev. Robert Mount; the Assistant Headmaster, Academic; the Assistant Headmaster, Administration; the Senior Housemaster; the Housemasters and Housemistresses; the Bursar; the Senior Prefect and his Assistants; the House Prefects; all the Security Guards on duty at the time of the incident; all other Security Guards at the school including the Chief Security Guard (they might have had a wind of the revolt). Do not forget that this list would not have been exhaustive enough. Other names could even have cropped up in the course of the investigation or elsewhere later.

After all interrogation, the writing of Statements and the gathering of sufficient evidence from other sources, we would have submitted a comprehensive report immediately to the appropriate authorities as required. The report would, of course, have contained an in depth analysis or assessment of the evidence obtained from which intelligent inferences and recommendations would have been made for the effective and efficient prevention of a recurrence of any such incident in the school.

We would have been <u>particularly mindful</u> of the facts that (i) ***"the student is not always wrong"*** and ***(ii) "the Headmaster may not necessarily have personally done any wrong thing that should make him the target*** *of the students' insurrection".* The students' action might have been justifiable; nevertheless it could be any side's case, who knows! We would therefore have ensured avoidance of all unprofessional attitudes including spicing our findings with speculation, emotions, personal interests and other biases - not passing judgement even before the start of the actual investigation.

CASE STUDY 11.

A whistle blower, Mercy ELLS, alerted the authorities of his home country, an Island in the Pacific Ocean, that a top politician in the House of Representatives possessed the International Passports of four different countries in addition to that of her home country. Her name was given as Mancel ERATA.

Now, the laws of that Island only permitted Dual Nationality but subject to Registration and approval by the Internal Affairs Ministry.

Supposing we were officials of that Island and such a case was referred to us to investigate and make appropriate recommendations to deal with similar situations in future, how would we go about it?

Possible Approach
As discussed earlier in this book, whenever there was the need to investigate any issue, one of the first things to do would be to ask ourselves: "What are we to establish or find out?" In other words, what exactly was required of the investigation? The correct identification of that from the formal information provided to us would constitute the premise for a good or successful planning of our work. Many investigators would sometimes miss this mark and so automatically end up producing bad jobs; in some cases they would even incur the wrath or displeasure of their superiors.

In the fore-going hypothesis, the investigator would be required to "Establish the Truth as to whether the legislator in question (Manuel ERATA) truly possessed passports of any foreign country or countries". Then other associated inquisitions such as how, when, where and why he acquired those passports, among others, could also be roped in. An allegation had only been made against her. It could be true or false.

So, as part of the planning, we would list:

a. What information we have;
b. What information we need to know; and from here we determine;
c. How and from where can we access the required information or evidence?

For (a), we have:

i.   The name of the legislator or suspect (Macel ERATA)
ii. The name of the whistle-blower (Mercy ELLS) we may or may not contact her for assistance, though in certain cases, the informant or source of the original allegation or report can be contacted for any leads and ambiguities.
iii. The exact allegation or "offence" (Possession of Passports of four different countries at the same time);

For (b), we may need to know:

i.   Is it true that Mancel ERATA possesses the Passports or Passports of any foreign country? And if true,
ii.   Which are these countries?
iii. Where are the said passports for proof?
iv.   Has Mancel ERATA ever used any of them to travel?, if yes,
v.   How often (how many times, when and from where to where and for what purposes).
vi.   Where did Mancel ERATA acquire each of these foreign passports, granted that she truly possessed any.
vii. Why did she acquire them and when? (Purpose or intent) The investigator may not need to ask direct questions here. Subtle means may be used to establish this.

We then come to (c), how do we access the unknown information? And from where?

At this stage we will first ask ourselves: "What type of Investigation are we going to adopt at all? Is it Open Investigation, Secret Investigation or both?

For this case, a little secret investigation may be useful to enable us gather some reliable information in respect of how Mancel ERATA acquired the respective foreign passports, if she did at all, and also to establish other supportive pieces of evidence including circumstantial ones.

Generally, Open Investigation would be required for this exercise. Earlier in this book, we saw "how to obtain evidence". For this scenario we shall use:

a. Interrogation
b. Interviews
c. Elicitation
d. Search
e. Examination of Documents (passports).

We shall interrogate the main suspect, Mancel ERATA. In the course of this if any other names crop up that need to throw more light on the issue at stake, we shall have to arrange to interrogate them as well. We may also have to interrogate Mercy ELLS, as a witness.

If it turns out for instance that Mancel ERATA ever travelled on any of these passports to and from her home country, then the appropriate local Immigration Officers at the points of departure or entry, as the case may be, will also have to be interrogated as witnesses, to provide the relevant evidence.

We may also have to carefully conduct Interviews and Elicitation on this allegation in the "environment" of Mancel ERATA. That includes her associates, workplace and family. Secret Investigation would be more appropriate here.

Irrespective of the social standing of the suspect, she must be very politely searched as a legal requirement of the investigation. This will cover her body, office, home, vehicle and other premises of hers for evidence. This is extremely important. The suspect may even be involved in a much worse offence than that which has come to security notice. It has to be stressed here that all such searches must be done within time and with decency.

Then, of course, should it be true that the legislator had any passport including that of her home country, they should all be technically examined for evidence that would enable the appropriate inferences to be drawn. Some of them may be fake passports. And, if so, then another full-scale investigation on the acquisition and supply of fake passports is on hand.

Every person interrogated would have to give a Statement immediately after each interrogation. (Don't forget the relevance of Independent Witnesses in these matters). Ordinary witnesses would have to be subjected to the same treatment. Even if technical or Electronic means were used to record interrogations or interviews, it is required of us to still obtain Statements from all persons interrogated. This is followed immediately by a Report. We may note here, and not only for this specific exercise, that it is unprofessional to shelve or delay Investigation Reports.

Investigation Reports should be written and presented to the appropriate authorities immediately after all possible evidence have been gathered. Where for very tangible reasons a full Report cannot be ready immediately, at least we always ensure that an "Interim Report" is promptly submitted on the findings so far. Such a Report should be labelled "Interim Report" on the subject matter.

It is also unprofessional for an investigator to orchestrate the delay of investigation Reports by, say, arranging with suspects/wanted persons or witnesses to stay away from or frustrate investigations just to delay investigation reports for calculated selfish/personal rewards or objectives. That is not good enough for this and any other investigation.

If in the investigation we came by some exhibits, these should be distinctly labelled, clearly referenced in the Report and carefully attached to it. Much care must be taken to preserve exhibits under Standard Temperatures and Pressures (STP) and in the original geometric conditions, as we saw under "Planning" in Chapter 2 of this book.

CASE STUDY 12.

Three armed robbers used an unmanned police barrier at WOEKE to rob traders on a Fante City-bound bus. According to the traders, the robbers barricaded the road as was usually done by the police and when the bus on which they were travelling got to the barrier, three men in black overall emerged from the darkness and ordered the driver and his mate out of the vehicle at gun point. They collected the driver's mobile phones and an amount of bH¢3,500 before firing into the vehicle and injuring three women in the process.

The robbers molested all persons on board the vehicle, including the injured women, before robbing them of their valuables.

On seeing a vehicle approaching from the direction of nearby Vegbe the robbers fled into the bush.

Three of the five injured traders were referred to the Prof. Smith Teaching Hospital, Accra, while two have since been discharged.

This robbery was the fifth in two weeks in the same area and thus calls for swift action to check the menace.

According to the report, four policemen at the WOEKE Police barrier on the VEGBE-HOLU road, where the robbery took place, in the Holu District of the Quodens Region of an island called Organn were on duty at the said barrier on Saturday, October 10, 2009. They were to fall out at 06.00 hours on Sunday October 11, 2009 but prematurely left their duty post at about 11.00 p.m. on Saturday, October 10,2009. Barely an hour later, the robbers struck using their base to rob travellers.

According to the local Police, two of the policemen were from the Xeyne Police Station and the others from Zinco Police Station. The Divisional Police Commander is reported to have ordered the immediate arrest of all the policemen in question, explaining that the measure was part of the resolve of the Police Administration to instil discipline and high professional standards among its personnel.

"Comment on this Report in relation to the Police", we are asked to.

Comments: (Note: The comments here are not necessarily exhaustive).

For the same crime to occur in the same area at such an alarming rate within such a short period of time, pre-supposes something has gone wrong especially on the part of the Investigators and/or those who are supposed to act on the investigation reports for each of the occasions that a robbery took place and came to security notice in the affected area. The problem could be caused by a number of factors, such as:

a. *Investigations* were not properly conducted into each of the robberies as they came to security notice and that in turn meant, among other things:
   (i) The truth surrounding the exact cause of each of the respective robberies was not well established; or
   (ii) the truth was established but not all evidence was embodied in the respective Investigation Reports; or
   (iii) the truth was established and fully embodied in the respective Investigation Reports but the Authorities flatly ignored them either for personal interests in the matter or slack in taking swift action on the Reports; or
   (iv) The truth was embodied in the Reports but no proper analysis of the evidence contained thereof could be made to come out with the appropriate recommendations to solve the problem; or
   (v) A proper analysis was made of the evidence available and the appropriate recommendations adduced by the respective investigators but the authorities failed, refused or were reluctant to take appropriate action on them.
b. The **Modus Operandi** of the robbers, for each of the robberies, was not, or could not, be determined or determined properly by investigators. For such reason, no good strategies could be formulated to check the robbery in the affected area and hence their recurrence there.

Other possibilities could be:

    c.   The Police on duty could be the robbers;

    d.   The duty Police themselves could be in league with the robbers.

Now, for each of (c) and (d) above, we will need to find out, among other things, when each of these robberies took place in the affected area, which specific Police personnel, including supervisors, were supposed to be on duty. It could be possible that one or two particular Police personnel would be the same people on duty anytime there was a robbery in the affected area. (Note, however, that this can only be circumstantial evidence).

From all the above reasons, and considering the gravity of the offence, especially being a serious threat to the Security of the area, urgent steps would have to be taken to restore a sound atmosphere there. There would, therefore, be the need to do the following:

1. Use fresh and more reliable investigators not from the same Station to conduct investigations into the latest robbery case (such investigators could come from the same Region, Division, District but not the same Station).

2. The fresh investigators should ensure they contact the right persons or sources for evidence, e.g. the injured traders, the driver and mate of each vehicle that was attacked, and persons living in and around the area where the robbery took place for information on any suspicious movements or presence of persons that may have come to anyone's notice there prior to, during and after the robbery;

3. A fresh duty roster, in respect of the affected duty post, has to be considered quickly and carefully too;

4. Establish the exact location of each of the duty Policemen, whose duty post was allegedly used by the robbers, at the time of the robbery:

5. Establish the circumstances that made all the duty Policemen at that particular duty post to fall out before the scheduled time. It could be they left the area for their personal safety because they had no weapons to protect themselves, no shelter from a threatening rainstorm, or some other phony excuses, and therefore felt insecure; perhaps earlier appeals to Superior Officers to even fix such personal security problems for duty personnel all fell on deaf ears.

6. Establish whether there had ever been formal complaints about difficulties pertaining to insecurity of personnel on duty especially at the barriers in the affected Divisional or District Police jurisdiction;

7. Find out who was the supervisor of duty personnel at the time of the robbery. Demand a full report covering the period he was supposed to be on duty as a Supervisor of duty personnel and which covers the time of the robbery;

8. Check the Station Diary to verify when each of the affected duty Police personnel correctly booked for duty, when each of them fell out of duty and for what reasons. Did they sign in for any ammunition and did they return same. If any losses, why?

9. Check their phones to determine calls made, received, and missed by each of the affected Policemen just before they went on duty, when they were on duty and after they fell out of duty;

10. Should the robbers be arrested, establish the relationship between each of the Policemen in question and every one of the robbers. This will require a separate full-scale investigation.

11. Visit the scene of the robbery (the unmanned police barrier where the robbery allegedly took place) and gather available pieces of evidence. Any spent cartridges? If yes, what type? Does the type match those supplied to the affected Policemen for their official duties on that fateful day?, and so on.

Finally, because of the need to determine the correct Modus Operandi of robbers in the area in question, it would be useful to re-examine all available investigation reports on the previous robberies in the area, especially within the past two weeks. From there, it might be easier to evolve efficient and effective strategies to safeguard the security of the area, at least in respect of armed robbery.

Many thanks for reading.

APPENDIX "A"

THE STATEMENT FORM

SECTION:_____

STATION:_____

DATE:_____

FULL NAME:_____

POSTAL ADDRESS:_____

HOUSE NO. :_____

NATIONALITY:_____

AGE:_____ SEX:_____

OCCUPATION:_____ PROFESSION:_____

HOME TOWN:_____ TRIBE: _____

TELEPHONE NO. :_____

E-MAIL ADDRESS (if any):_____

_____

_____

_____

APPENDIX "B"

CAUTION WORDS AND ACKNOWLEDGEMENT

(i)   SUSPECT CAUTION WORDS

A case of ___{**briefly state the exact suspected offence or offences here**}___ in which you are suspected of involvement is under investigation. That you are not obliged to say anything unless you wish to do so and that whatever you say shall be recorded in writing and same tendered in evidence against you. You are entitled to counsel of your own choice.

_____

Signature, Full Name, Rank/Title of
Investigator Date and Time.

_____

Signature/Right Thumb-Print (RTP),
Full Name of suspect, Date and Time.

_____

Signature/RTP of Independent Witness, Full Name
Address, Telephone, Date and Time.

The acknowledgement begins immediately here:

ACKNOWLEDGEMENT (SUSPECT)

I have been told that a case of _____{**briefly quote the suspected offence or offences here**}_____ in which I am suspected of involvement is under investigation. That I am not obliged to say anything unless I wish to do so and that whatever I say shall be recorded in writing and same tendered in evidence against me. I have also been told of my right to counsel of my own choice.

_____

Suspect's signature/RTP, Full Name,
Date & Time

_____

Signature, Full Name, Rank of Investigator,
Date And Time.

_____

Signature/RTP of Independent Witness, Full Name
Address, Telephone, Date & Time.

(ii)   NOTE: The same holds for **Accused Caution Statement** and its Acknowledgement, except that the expression "*suspect of involvement*" gives way to "*INVOLVED*" as we saw earlier in this book.

ABOUT THE AUTHOR

This Author is an internationally trained professional in Intelligence, Counter-Intelligence and Criminal Investigation and served the Government of Ghana in these capacities for over twenty years.

E. Anim-Danquah is also the author of "PRINCIPLES OF INTERROGATION", published in the USA; "A HANDBOOK ON INVESTIGATION" and "THE ART OF INVESTIGATION", published in Ghana.

He was a lecturer in intelligence and investigation at the Ghana Immigration Service Academy and Training School concurrently for four years.

He is now into private business.

Email: ghanass73@gmail.com
Tel.: +233-244-954-957 / +233-263-902-721.

www.ingramcontent.com/pod-product-compliance
Lightning Source LLC
Chambersburg PA
CBHW030429290526
45786CB00001B/200